HOW TO DEAL WITH YOUR LAWYER: ANSWERS TO COMMONLY ASKED QUESTIONS

by

Lawrence J. Fox and Susan R. Martyn

Oceana's Legal Almanac Series:
Law for the Layperson

Oceana®
NEW YORK

OXFORD

UNIVERSITY PRESS

Oxford University Press, Inc., publishes works that further Oxford University's objective of excellence in research, scholarship, and education.

Copyright © 2008 by Oxford University Press, Inc.
Published by Oxford University Press, Inc.
198 Madison Avenue, New York, New York 10016

Library of Congress Cataloging-in-Publication Data

Fox, Lawrence J., 1943-
  How to deal with your lawyer : answers to commonly asked questions / by Lawrence J. Fox and Susan R. Martyn.
    p. cm. -- (Oceana's legal almanac series : law for the layperson)
  Includes index.
  ISBN-13: 978-0-19-537077-5 (alk. paper) 1. Attorney and client--United States--Popular works. 2. Practice of law--United States--Popular works.
I. Martyn, Susan R., 1947- II. Title.
  KF311.F69 2008
  347.73'504--dc22   2007052460

Note to Readers:

> You may order this or any other Oxford University Press publication by visiting the Oxford University Press website at www.oup.com

To Juliet Maeve and Vivienne Reece

Table of Contents

PART THREE:
WHAT NOT TO EXPECT FROM YOUR LAWYER

PART FOUR:
OTHER PEOPLE'S LAWYERS

PART FIVE:
GAINING EVEN WHEN YOU LOSE

ABOUT THE AUTHORS

Lawrence J. Fox practices law as a long-time partner at Drinker Biddle & Reath. Larry is the I. Grant Irey Adjunct Professor of Law at the University of Pennsylvania and a Lecturer on Law at the Harvard Law School, where he teaches students professional responsibility. Larry chaired the ABA Ethics Committee which is responsible for the drafting and interpretation of lawyer rules of conduct. Larry also teaches professional responsibility to practicing lawyers in continuing legal education courses held around the country. The United States State Department sent Larry to Argentina and China to instruct lawyers and judges in those two countries on lawyer and judicial ethics. He has appeared on the television shows *CNN Crossfire, Nightline, MSNBC* and the *Today Show*.

Susan R. Martyn has taught law for nearly thirty years, first at Wayne State University in Detroit, and currently as Stoepler Professor of Law and Values at the University of Toledo College of Law. She specializes in legal ethics and has authored four books and more than thirty articles in scholarly journals. Susan's teaching and writing flow out of her service on several national advisory bodies in the past fifteen years that have shaped the law governing lawyer conduct. She and Larry acted as advisors to the American Law Institute's Restatement of the Law Governing Lawyers (1987–2000), and they were two of thirteen members of the American Bar Association's Ethics 2000 Commission (1997–2002). Susan currently serves on the ABA's Standing Committee on Ethics and Professional Responsibility.

ACKNOWLEDGMENTS

Our collaboration started with the preparation of a casebook for law students, *Traversing the Ethical Minefield: Problems, Law and Professional Responsibility* (Aspen Publishers 2004). We are grateful for the continuing response of law students to these materials, which has encouraged us to write for other audiences. We branched out and spoke to practicing lawyers in our second publication, *Red Flags: A Lawyer's Handbook on Legal Ethics* (ALI-ABA 2005). Once again, we have been blessed with feedback from lawyers who seem to appreciate our attempt to make legal ethics fun and intelligible. In this Almanac, we have rounded out our attempts to make the law governing lawyer conduct accessible by speaking directly to the most important audience of all: clients.

Of course, no volume like this would be possible without the extraordinary assistance of many, especially since we are lawyers and need to be reminded about our tendency to lapse into legal jargon. We thank the following non-lawyer reviewers who helped make clear to us that legal writing can be to clear writing as military music is to music. Bea Cucinotta, your dedicated reading of this manuscript, devotion to detail and consistency continues to amaze us. Kelly Kszywienski, Carol Stacy, Melissa Hicks and Peter Martyn, your comments about the overall tone and message of the Almanac helped us reshape our language. Ralph DeGroff, Jr., your dedication to precise use of language is the stuff of legends.

PREFACE

The American public spends dearly each year on legal services. And those legal services are provided to handle the very most important matters clients face—the purchase of a home and other important transactions, wills, custody issues and divorce, any time a client has to go to court. Yet as important as a client's entry onto the legal terrain may be, more often than not it is a trip through unfamiliar territory without a map or a compass. While in an ideal world each lawyer could be counted on to share this information face-to-face with each new client, the truth is that this does not always occur. And, as far as we know, there is no guide that provides clients with the information they need about what their lawyers owe them. We hope this Almanac will provide both the map and the compass.

Our purpose here is to provide you with the information you should know about the ethical obligations of your lawyer. While this Almanac is no substitute for informed conversation between your counsel and you (itself an ethical requirement), as one famous retailer observes, "An informed consumer is our best customer." The more clients know about these matters, the more likely clients' encounters with lawyers and our legal system will be rewarding ones.

We hope that you will read this Almanac in that spirit. We invite you to chuckle with us at the cartoons designed to illustrate topics in each chapter. We've also included boxes that outline the highlights of each chapter and provide you with questions you can and should ask your lawyer about a particular topic. Finally, we call your attention to the bolded terms in the volume, which mean that we have defined them in a glossary at the end of the Almanac. We hope all of this information will not only educate clients, but, indirectly, will promote a higher level of ethical conduct in the lawyers you hire.

PART ONE

THE CLIENT-LAWYER RELATIONSHIP

INTRODUCTION

In this part of the Almanac, we begin by exploring some of the ethical and legal regulation that reminds lawyers of the special nature of the client-lawyer relationship. We also offer you tips on finding and paying a lawyer.

We know the jokes. The suggestions that "lawyers' ethics" is just another oxymoron like military justice. The fact is that because we serve clients, lawyers are required to abide by a rather elaborate code of conduct designed to protect client interests.

No lawyer in America may practice law until he or she has been admitted to the bars of one or more states or the District of Columbia. Historically and literally, "admitted to the bar" means that a lawyer has permission to appear in courts, on the side of the "bar" or rail nearest the judge. But today, bar admission also grants a lawyer permission to draft legal documents and give legal advice. Court appearances also have grown to include representing clients in **arbitration**, **mediation**, and other forms of **alternative dispute resolution**.

Each state and the District of Columbia controls its own bar admission, generally through the state's Supreme Court. And once a lawyer is admitted, each state also imposes **Rules of Professional Conduct** with which each lawyer must agree to comply, a code that, if violated, can result in the sanctioning—even the suspension or disbarment—of the offending lawyer.

But enough of dwelling on the potential downside of the profession. The purpose of this little volume is positive. We want you to understand how these **Rules of Professional Conduct** shape the client-lawyer relationship, by requiring lawyers to observe what we call the "4 Cs": **communication, competence, confidentiality,** and **conflict of interest** resolution. We explain these professional obligations of lawyers in the first eight chapters.

In the rest of the book, we offer guidance about what not to expect from your lawyer (Chapter 9), how to deal with other people's lawyers (Chapter 10) and how to evaluate your legal representation (Chapter 11).

HOW DO LAWYERS DIFFER FROM OTHER SERVICE PROVIDERS?

1. Admission: A lawyer cannot offer legal services unless he or she is admitted to practice law in each state where he or she regularly practices. To be admitted to the bar, each lawyer must:
  a. Graduate from a recognized law school
  b. Pass a bar exam
  c. Establish personal character through a lengthy background check, and
  d. Take an oath.
2. Once admitted, each lawyer must follow that state's **Rules of Professional Conduct**. Each code regulates:
  a. The client-lawyer relationship, including **the 4 Cs:**
    i. **Competence**
    ii. **Communication**
    iii. **Confidentiality** and
    iv. **Conflict of interest** resolution
  b. The lawyer's duties to the courts
  c. The lawyer's duties to other third persons

CHAPTER 1:
WHAT MAKES THE CLIENT-LAWYER
RELATIONSHIP SO SPECIAL?

The typical American buys goods and services from hundreds of different vendors. Think of a typical week and you will interact with dozens—getting a haircut, buying groceries, washing your car, taking out a loan, filling a cavity, getting gas, parking, making car payments—the list is endless. What makes your dealings with a lawyer so different or special? It is not that the lawyer is a privileged character worthy of special awe and respect; rather it is the reverse. In your dealings with a lawyer, it is you, the client, who is entitled to receive special treatment. Your lawyer is only special because the lawyer has special responsibilities to you.

Your lawyer owes you a **fiduciary duty**. That is a 10-dollar phrase that means that your lawyer must put your interests ahead of his or hers. This does not mean your lawyer may not charge for her services; but if she does charge, the **fee** must be reasonable, not whatever the traffic will bear. It does not mean that you are the lawyer's only client. But if your lawyer takes on other clients, she must assure you that your interests are not compromised by her commitment to another client, a former client or his own self-interest.

It does mean that your lawyer must provide you with **the 4 Cs**: **communication**, **competence**, **confidentiality** and **conflict of interest** resolution. Your lawyer must initiate **communication** with you to give you the opportunity to control the ongoing course of the representation. You are entitled to a **competent** lawyer who can guide you through the maze of unfamiliar law you need to navigate. To offer **competent** advice, your lawyer must learn all she can about the matter and therefore must keep your confidences, and not disclose those confidences to third parties or use them to your disadvantage. Finally, it does mean that your lawyer must be loyal and ever vigilant to other interests that might compromise her judgment on your behalf. This means that your lawyer must segregate and safeguard your property, and that your lawyer must act in your best interests, not her self-interest or the interests of any other person.

A LAWYER'S FIDUCIARY DUTY: THE 4 Cs

1. *Communication*: Your lawyer must explain:
    a. Information you need to know
    b. The fee
    c. The scope of the representation, or what the lawyer intends to do for you
    d. Any **conflicts of interest**
2. *Competence*: Your lawyer must:
    a. Know the law and legal procedures
    b. Prepare thoroughly
    c. Follow-through promptly
3. *Confidentiality*: Your lawyer must protect all information relating to the representation
4. *Conflict of Interest Resolution*: Your lawyer must:
    a. Check for conflicts
    b. Disclose any conflicts arising from interests of the lawyer, **law firm**, other clients or former clients of the firm
    c. Obtain your consent to conflicts before proceeding.

There are elaborate rules to give real meaning and structure to these and other important principles. But more important than these detailed rules is the overarching principle that your lawyer has special responsibilities to you that should be viewed not as some side benefit or frill, but as the very hallmark of your relationship. You should feel that your lawyer is your one true champion. If your lawyer does not convey that commitment, then it is time to re-examine the relationship or exercise your right at any time, for any reason or for no reason at all, to fire your lawyer and find one who will meet the standards of commitment to which you are entitled.

"Edna, this is Frank, my happiness, solace, delight, inspiration, comfort, joy, and lawyer."

CHAPTER 2:
FINDING A LAWYER

This Almanac assumes you have already found a lawyer and want to know what to expect from your lawyer of choice. But it could be that you are reading this book before you have chosen a lawyer. If so, a few tips should help you along the way.

LAWYERS MAY ADVERTISE (UP TO A POINT); LAWYERS MAY SOLICIT (UP TO A POINT)

Q: *The phone book is filled with ads. I see some on television, too. How does one choose?*

A: Think of how you last found a dentist. Responding to ads might not be the best way to proceed. You might want to try to call friends for a personal referral. On the other hand, some of the most capable and honorable lawyers advertise extensively. And lawyers' advertisements are tightly monitored by the bar for compliance with the profession's ethical guidelines.

Lawyers are not permitted to advertise results that could be misleading. No two cases are alike. Just because a lawyer snared $100,000 for client A doesn't mean that $100,000 was an outstanding result (maybe the case should have resulted in a $250,000 recovery) or that the lawyer will get you that sum (your claim may be weaker ... or much stronger). They may not use endorsements by rock stars, politicians, former clients, or anyone else that could create an unjustified expectation. They may not promise results. They must describe their **fee arrangements** accurately.

So it is perfectly acceptable to use advertisements as a way of deciding which lawyers to contact, but do not use ads as a basis for selecting a lawyer. Preferably, you should not select a lawyer until you have interviewed several lawyers, evaluated them face to face, and assured yourself that the lawyers you are meeting are the lawyers who will actually provide your legal services. The lawyer you select should be the person you are willing to trust with what might be the most sensitive and important matter you've ever dealt with, one who has sufficient experience, drive and good judgment to tackle your problem, and one whose proposed **fee arrangement** is satisfactory to you.

Q: *If I don't know any lawyers, how can I get a personal referral? To tell you the truth the whole thing scares me.*

A: Your feelings are not unique. It is the lawyers' responsibility to set you at ease. And just because you don't know any lawyers is no reason not to seek a referral. Your friends and neighbors may know lawyers. Maybe someone at work has a lawyer he or she can recommend. Don't forget that when your lazy brother-in-law got hurt at work, the lawyer he hired got him enough money to buy your sister a mink coat.

Q: *But those people didn't face the same kind of problem I have.*

A: That may be so. But using their contacts in the profession—assuming your friends were satisfied with their lawyers—is a better way to gain access to the system than comparing Yellow Pages ads or TV commercials. And if these lawyers are not experts in your matter, they will be in a good position to make an excellent referral. In fact, to encourage referrals, we allow referring lawyers to collect a referral **fee** from the lawyer they recommend.

Q: *So if I go to a lawyer and my problem is one he can't handle, he'll tell me that?*

A: That's one possibility. Another is for the lawyer to associate with another lawyer with more experience. You are entitled to know if the first lawyer does that. And, as noted, the lawyer also can refer you to another lawyer. In that case, the lawyer who makes the referral might get a referral fee.

Q: *Sounds unsavory to me.*

A: Not really. It encourages lawyers to refer matters when the matter is one where a specialist is in your best interests. And, in order to get a referral fee, the lawyer must continue to share responsibility for the matter. You must be informed of the amount or percentage of the referral fee. And the overall **fee** you pay must be reasonable.

Q: *Can I get advice on where to go for help without calling a lawyer?*

A: In many cities there are lawyer referral services that will recommend lawyers in various fields. Some unions and other organizations have a recommended list of lawyers. But in all of these circumstances, we recommend that you meet with more than one lawyer before you decide whom to hire.

Q: *I was involved in a little bus accident last month. Not really hurt, but I got this letter from a lawyer wanting to represent me. Says I'll get big bucks.*

A: Lawyers' **solicitation** of clients used to be limited by the law. But in the last three decades, the United States Supreme Court struck down most limitations on written but not oral **communications**. So it is perfectly all right for a lawyer to solicit you directly by mail. Of course, the letter has to be truthful and not make promises of how successful the lawyer will be. The one thing you can't be subjected to is an in-person **solicitation**. We still prohibit lawyers from walking the hospital halls, signing up accident victims still groggy from Demerol.

QUESTIONS TO ASK A LAWYER ABOUT QUALIFICATIONS

1. *General Qualifications:*
   a. Where are you admitted to practice?
   b. What law school did you graduate from? When?
   c. Have you ever been subject to **professional discipline?**
   d. Do you have **malpractice** insurance?

2. *Specific Qualifications:*
   a. How many matters like mine have you handled?
   b. What happened in those cases?
   c. How will you handle my situation?
   d. How would other lawyers handle my situation?
   e. Based on your experience, what can I reasonably expect?
   f. Will you be the lawyer working on my matter?
   g. Will there be any limitations on the scope of your representation?
   h. Are there any alternatives to what you have recommended, such as **mediation** or handling the matter on my own?

LAWYERS MAY SPECIALIZE

Q: *When I have a sore shoulder, I go to an orthopedist; when my child is depressed, I take him to a psychiatrist; but lawyers all seem to be general practitioners. How do I know the lawyer I go to knows how to do what I need to have done?*

A: A lawyer's license to practice permits him to undertake any engagement. But there are two things you should know. First, lawyers are required by the **Rules of Professional Conduct** to be **competent**. If the work your lawyer undertakes for you is a specialized area of the law—tax, securities, **litigation**—his performance will be judged by the standards of those who specialize in this work. That requirement discourages lawyers from taking on matters with which they are unfamiliar.

Second, in some states lawyers are permitted to advertise and otherwise inform you that they have been certified, by virtue of their experience and testing, in a particular specialty. While such certifications are no guarantee of the quality of services you will receive, those who certify these lawyers are vigorously regulated, and they usually require more education and experience and passing an examination in a specialized area of law.

REFERRALS BY LAWYERS

Q: *My lawyer is helping me with my estate plan. He recommended life insurance and a particular agent—some guy with an office down the hall. Is that kosher?*

A: Lawyers have to maintain their independence when it comes to making or receiving referrals. It's okay for lawyers to have good reciprocal relationships with money managers and life insurance sales people, but they always must make referrals that are in the best interests of the client. A lawyer can never enter into exclusive referral arrangements with any vendor, and if your lawyer does make a referral to an insurance agent who makes referrals back to him, he must disclose that fact to you and remind you that there are other vendors you might want to consider.

Q: *I always wondered why lawyers didn't bring all these other law-related services into their **law firms** so we clients could have one-stop shopping: Real estate advice, mortgage financing, title insurance, environmental testing.*

A: On the surface, it sounds like a good idea. But our profession has decided that lawyers might lose their professional independence if the **law firm** were a profit center for other services and lawyers ended up influenced by non-lawyers who don't have all the obligations we outline in this book.

Q: *There you go acting as if lawyers are better than everyone else.*

A: Some say that—but not the authors. It is true that lawyers carry special burdens, but we also can be all too human. These rules against profit sharing with non-lawyers just eliminate a little temptation—all for your benefit. Believe us; lawyers could earn more money if they could operate one-stop shops. They, of course, could lose more, too.

"Ladies and gentlemen, is there a bankruptcy attorney on board?"

CHAPTER 3:
PAYING A LAWYER

YOUR LAWYERS' FEES MUST BE FULLY EXPLAINED

Q: *My sense is lawyers love to charge big bucks, but don't like talking about it much.*

A: You are right there. But even before you become a client, you are entitled to a number of protections regarding **fees**. Your lawyer must discuss the available methods of billing—**hourly fee**, **fixed fee**, **contingent fee**—and the benefits and drawbacks of each.

Q: *Tell me more about hourly billing.*

A: This is the most common way lawyers charge. Each lawyer and **paralegal** has a billing rate. They are supposed to keep accurate track of their time, usually in fractions of an hour, and describe what they do during that time. Then, at the end of the month, the lawyer will send you a bill containing the descriptions and the important mathematical result.

Q: *What's that?*

A: The number of hours times the billable rate for each individual who dedicated time to the matter, all neatly added up.

Q: *Couldn't this be a great deal for the lawyer? She works real slow and I pay for every hour.*

A: That's where reasonableness comes in—and a lawyer's **fiduciary duty**. Your lawyer is required to proceed efficiently and pursue only those objectives you have agreed to, following the strategic plan you two have discussed.

Q: *How will I ever know?*

A: You are right to ask. This system is built on trust and documentation. You are not sitting around watching your lawyer's every move, stopwatch in hand. But if you don't trust your lawyer, billing is only part of the problem, and you would be well served to keep searching until you find one you do trust.

Q: *What's this about fixed fees?*

A: Sometimes lawyer and client can agree that the lawyer will provide all services required for a **fixed fee**, if the service is routine, or the lawyer and client have a large database of experience with this type of matter.

Q: *Sounds like this could be an incentive for slipshod work.*

A: With any **fixed fee**, we're back to trust again—and the recognition by the lawyer that a **malpractice** action might loom if she does not deliver quality work.

Q: *And if it takes longer, the lawyer might lose interest?*

A: That's certainly possible. You've now identified the problems with **fixed fees**. But they have their place and they permit the client the benefit of budgeting for the cost of these services, which can be quite reassuring in the right circumstances. So the ethics rules generally permit them, except in one instance.

Q: *What's that?*

A: Many jurisdictions prohibit **fixed fees** in situations in which the lawyer is hired by an insurance company to represent an insured who is the real client. The worry is that the lawyer's professional independence will be compromised by the arrangement, so rather than worry about it, **fixed fees** are just prohibited.

Q: *I've also heard about **contingent fees**. How do they work?*

A: These are arrangements that we say hold the keys to the courthouse door for so many who otherwise could not afford lawyers.

Q: *How's that?*

A: Under a **contingent fee arrangement**, the lawyer collects a **fee** only if the client has a recovery. And the **fee** is directly tied to the amount of the recovery. The more the client gets, the more the lawyer gets. Those interests are really perfectly aligned.

Q: *That sounds great. Why doesn't everyone hire a lawyer on a **contingent fee**?*

A: Well, first of all, even in cases that are appropriate for **contingent fees**, lawyers are required to explain the alternatives to the client since some clients certainly would prefer to pay a lawyer on some other basis.

How to Deal With Your Lawyer

Then there are some matters where the law prohibits **contingent fees**, primarily divorces and criminal matters; the former because we always hope a lawyer's **fee arrangement** would not discourage a desired reconciliation and the latter because we don't want the **fee** agreement to interfere with the client's ability to accept a plea bargain.

Q: *How much is the lawyer's percentage?*

A: Again, we are back to reasonable. Typically, lawyers will charge anywhere from 25 to 40%. But in cases where recovery is more certain, such a high percentage might be unreasonable. And the percentage does not have to be fixed across all recoveries. Some states have legislated what the percentages shall be in certain cases, and those percentages may go down as recoveries go up. For example, the lawyer gets one-third of the first $100,000; 25% on the next $100,000; 10% on anything over $200,000. Others have endorsed **contingent fee arrangements** where the percentage rises as the recovery increases on the theory that the last dollar recovered is a much better accomplishment than recovering the first.

Q: *So under a **contingent fee**, I get my lawyer for free?*

A: Well, the legal services are free, if you should lose. But we haven't discussed **expenses**, which includes everything from court filing **fees** and expert witness charges to costs for **disbursements**, such as phone calls and photocopy **expenses**.

Q: *There's always a catch.*

A: That's because the amount a client pays for every matter has two components: the professional **fee** and the **expenses**. Lawyers are allowed to include **expenses** in the **contingent fee**, which means that you don't pay them anything—**fee** or **expenses**—unless you win. Lawyers also are allowed to charge you for these **expenses** separately. Either way, you have a right to bargain for and know up front what to expect.

Q: *What is the issue about these charges?*

A: First, let's just identify some of what we are talking about: copying and telephone charges, electronic research, travel, meals, deposition transcripts, and similar items. Lawyers may do two things: Tell you the basis on which you will be charged—25¢/page for photocopying; $35/hr. for electronic research—or undertake elaborate cost accounting so that the provision of these services does not become an undisclosed profit center for the **law firm**. As to these and all other **expenses**, the lawyer in every representation must fully explain to you the basis on which these items will be charged, and, in the case of **contingent fee** matters, whether the client still has to pay the **expenses** apart from the **contingent fee** itself. The smart lawyers will set this all out in writing.

QUESTIONS TO ASK A LAWYER ABOUT FEES AND EXPENSES

1. What kind of fee do you recommend?
   a. If an **hourly fee**:
      i. How much do you charge per hour?
      ii. How many hours do you estimate my case will take?
      iii. What **expenses** might be required?
      iv. What happens if my case takes much longer than you estimate?
   b. If flat or **fixed fee**:
      i. How much time do these cases typically take you?
      ii. What **expenses** might be required?
      iii. What happens if my case suddenly settles tomorrow?
      iv. What happens if my matter takes twice as long as you expect?
   c. If a **contingent fee**:
      i. How likely is it I will recover?
      ii. How much do you estimate I might recover?
      iii. What percent contingency fee do you charge?
      iv. What percent fee do most lawyers in town charge?
      v. What **expenses** might be required?
      vi. What happens if my case suddenly settles tomorrow?
2. What alternative fees are possible?
3. What are the advantages and disadvantages of each kind of fee?
4. Can we agree to a **blended fee**, for example:
   a. An **hourly fee** with an upper limit?
   b. A **contingent fee** with a sliding scale, or one that begins or ends at a set amount?
   c. A flat fee combined with a **contingent fee** for recovery or savings over a certain amount?
5. Will you put our fee agreement in writing?
6. What kind of costs and **expenses** apart from fees do you expect in my case?
7. How will these costs be calculated?
8. Will our agreement regarding these costs be in writing?

Q: *Don't all fee arrangements have to be in writing?*

A: It depends on where you live. All **contingent fee** agreements must be in writing. So must all **fee** agreements in some states, but not everywhere. Nonetheless, the wise client will ask for a written retainer agreement and, if you ask, the lawyer must give you one. The whole exercise helps both lawyer and client, particularly if they get into a dispute about the **fee**. Not only will the lawyer provide you with a clear statement of the basis for the **fee**, but she will also make it clear to the client what is expected from the client as the matter goes forward.

Q: *Wait. I thought all I had to do was bring my legal matter to my lawyer.*

A: That, of course, is necessary, but not sufficient; clients have responsibilities too. They must cooperate with their lawyers: tell the lawyers what they need to know, provide documents as required, show up at meetings, depositions, court appearances, and … need we mention it? Pay their bills on time.

Q: *What happens if, after my lawyer and I agree on a fee, my lawyer then decides the deal still isn't to her liking?*

A: Great question. While clients can terminate lawyers at any time for any reason, a lawyer may not change a **fee** agreement previously entered into because "the deal" doesn't look as good as it once did. The courts look at any **fee** modification with significant disfavor. Unless the lawyer can demonstrate that the scope of the engagement materially changed or that it was otherwise in the client's best interest to change the arrangement, the lawyer must fulfill the terms of the original retainer.

YOUR LAWYERS' FEES MUST BE REASONABLE

The lawyer's duty does not end when she explains the nature of various **fee** agreements. There also are elaborate requirements regarding the substance of lawyer **fees**. The first principle is the lawyer's **fee** must be reasonable.

Q: *I know this one's a joke. All you lawyers are the same: you charge as much as the market will bear.*

A: We admit that some lawyers' ideas about what is **reasonable** may stretch the rules, but there really are limits to what lawyers may charge and lawyers' **fees** are always subject to scrutiny under that standard.

Q: *What do you mean?*

A: Clients may assert that their lawyers' **fees** are unreasonable at any time. Then a court or arbitrator will decide whether that is the case.

Q: *But "reasonable"—what a meaningless word.*

A: Not entirely. The lawyer codes list a number of factors that courts should consider. They all don't apply to every case, but determining whether the **fee** is **reasonable** by looking at the talent and experience of the lawyers, the results they achieved, the reasonableness of the lawyers' hourly rates, the risk associated with any contingency, and other listed factors makes the required inquiry much more objective than you may think.

YOUR LAWYER MUST SAFEGUARD YOUR PROPERTY

Lawyers have special obligations when it comes to safeguarding the property that is entrusted to them. These obligations exist because so often it is helpful for the lawyer to take custody of money and other valuables, and knowing that lawyers take this responsibility seriously can give clients extra peace of mind.

Q: *Could you give me some examples?*

A: A lawyer might hold a security deposit on a real estate purchase pending the sale, or receive the proceeds of the settlement of **litigation** pending court approval, or take custody of disputed jewelry or paintings pending a divorce.

Q: *So what does my lawyer do with this money?*

A: Your lawyer must keep your money and other valuables safe and separate from her own funds and property. This requires careful bookkeeping. Lawyers are required to maintain **client trust accounts**, and they may not mix or commingle their own money with their client's funds. If the sums are relatively small and will be held for a short period of time, the lawyer will put these funds in what is called an **IOLTA** account where any interest earned is used to pay for public interest endeavors. If the funds in custody are large or will be in the care of the lawyer for a significant period of time, a separate account must be established with any interest credited to the client.

Q: *Do lawyers get paid to do this?*

A: Lawyers are rarely compensated for these services. And if something goes wrong, the lawyer can only get in trouble.

*"I'm certain I speak for the entire legal profession when
I say that the fee is reasonable and just."*

PART TWO

WHAT TO EXPECT FROM YOUR LAWYER

In this part of the Almanac, we further explore **the 4 Cs**: your lawyer's obligation to **communicate**, be **competent**, keep your **confidences** and resolve any **conflicts of interest**.

CHAPTER 4:
YOUR LAWYER MUST COMMUNICATE
WITH YOU

As our **fee** discussion demonstrates, this is your lawyer's first obligation to you. You must be kept informed, so that your lawyer will represent your best interests as you define them. There is a fundamental obligation your lawyer undertakes that starts before the representation begins. Your lawyer must **communicate** with you about the scope of the representation, whether he has any possible **conflicts of interest**, how he expects to be paid, and any information you need to know to decide whether to hire him.

Q: *Sure. They **communicate** real well when they're trying to impress a new client. But I wonder how long that devotion lasts?*

A: Now, we won't deceive you; sometimes lawyers will shirk this responsibility. It may be because they're too busy, because they forget, or, we hate to admit this, because they find you to be a nuisance. But the reality does not change the obligation. You are entitled to two levels of **communication**.

First, you are entitled to periodic reports. Even if nothing is happening, from time to time you should hear from your lawyer. Second, if anything important happens, your lawyer should notify you immediately.

Q: *Yeah, but the lawyer gets to decide what's important.*

A: Not really. Your lawyer's obligation is to keep you advised of all material developments. It's what you, the client, would think is important.

Q: *So the lawyer tells me about "developments." Then the lawyer can go on his merry way. May as well not bother.*

A: That's not correct at all. From the very beginning of the representation the lawyer must not only **communicate** with you, but secure your input.

Q: *How do you mean?*

A: You come to a lawyer. You have a problem. You have a dream. You talk with your lawyer, tell him about your hopes and fears and then, after he lays out the possibilities, it is you—not your lawyer—who gets to decide what the scope of the representation should be. We say the client gets to decide the objectives and then it's the lawyer's job to carry them out.

Q: *So I can come to a lawyer and say I'll hire you for one hour, so that I don't end up paying an arm and a leg?*

A: Well, not quite. Lawyers can be hired for small matters or even to advise on a part of a matter. What we are not allowed to do is agree to a limitation in a representation that creates a restriction on meaningful legal services. Say you have a tax problem and to give good advice would take 10 hours. A lawyer cannot agree to provide one hour of services. But if you want to have a lawyer evaluate a proposed property settlement in a no-fault divorce, without addressing issues relating to child visitation, a lawyer can agree to that limitation.

Q: *But beyond that, it doesn't sound like I get to decide much.*

A: Au contraire. Beyond objectives, the client gets to decide all of the major strategic decisions. Should you make an offer now? Should you insist on a non-compete clause? Should you take someone's deposition? Hire an expert? File a counterclaim? All those decisions and a myriad more are for you to decide after consultation with your lawyer.

Q: *Consultation? What does that mean? I'll bet that doesn't take long. My lawyer tells me what to do and expects me to approve.*

A: Actually, consultation means much more. On major decisions—like whether to settle, whether to waive privilege, whether to agree to let your firm take on a conflicting representation—your lawyer must make sure he gets consent from you. That requires your lawyer to explain your choices, the ramifications of going one way or another, and any downsides so that your agreement is based on a full understanding of all the implications of the discussion.

Q: *And the rest the lawyer gets to decide on his own?*

A: Not true. Even on the means of achieving your objectives, a lawyer should consult with his client. It is true that day-to-day matters must not always be decided in consultation with the client—granting extensions of time to the other side, for example—but it's your matter and your money, so you get to decide.

Q: *I don't want my lawyer granting the other side extensions.*

A: If your matter is an emergency, you may be able to control your lawyer's ability to do so. But absent that, there is a sphere of matters where the lawyer, not the client, can exercise reasonably unfettered discretion.

QUESTIONS TO ASK A LAWYER ABOUT COMMUNICATION
1. How will you keep me informed about my case?
a. Will there be periodic reports? When?
b. When something important happens, will you notify me immediately?
2. How will you respond to my questions?
a. Should I call or email you?
b. Someone else?
c. Will you charge me for these questions?
3. How will we decide what to do and how to do it?

Q: *And if the lawyer was hired by the insurance company to defend me in that auto accident, then the insurance company gets to decide?*

A: No. No matter who is paying the lawyer—dad, to represent son, company, to represent employee, insurance company, to represent insured—the lawyer takes direction from the client, not the check-writer. We actually have two rules that make that clear: The first prevents interference in the client-lawyer relationship by requiring that your lawyer keep your confidences, tell you who is paying the bills, and get your consent to the arrangement. The second requires that your lawyer not permit the third party to direct or regulate his professional judgment on your behalf throughout the representation.

Q: *Maybe you have two rules because the insurance companies ignore the rule.*

A: It is true that the language of the rule is more pristine than the practice. Insurance companies will always want to control "their" money. And when they really are the only ones on the line, that may be okay. But when push comes to shove and the client has real interests on the line, the lawyer better act at the direction of the client, or both lawyer and insurance company could be in real trouble.

Q: *I sure don't want the insurance company deciding whether to settle that totally frivolous accident claim. The other driver was speeding.*

A: Not to worry. The lawyer is your lawyer. If you tell him not to settle, he cannot settle. Of course, you'll have to live with the consequences.

Q: *I knew you were talking out of both sides of your mouth.*

A: Not as to your lawyer. For example, some insurance policies entitle the insurance company to settle. If you direct the lawyer not to settle, he won't; but the insurance company can assert that the policy is now void and you are on your own. That won't be your lawyer's fault.

Q: *Say I'm suing some guy for injuries I suffered in an auto accident. What if I don't want to settle and my lawyer does?*

A: You get to decide. Your lawyer is entitled and indeed even required to give you his best advice. But if you choose to ignore your lawyer's advice to settle, he must continue to pursue the claim and vice versa. That's one of the contingencies your lawyer accepted when the two of you entered into a **contingent fee** agreement.

Q: *I know one thing my lawyer won't* **communicate**: *if he makes a mistake.*

A: Wrong again. Maybe the drug company doesn't have to tell you the latest tests show risk of ulcers, or the automobile manufacturer doesn't need to notify you the transmissions develop slippage. But the lawyer's duty of **communication** requires you to be notified of any lawyer errors, even those that might mean the lawyer is subject to a **malpractice** claim by you. It doesn't mean the lawyer will write you a check. But it does mean the lawyer will tell you of the mistake and advise you to seek further advice from another lawyer on how to proceed because your lawyer now has one big conflict with you.

Q: *What else?*

A: Your lawyer is permitted, but not required, to provide you with advice about matters other than law that come to the lawyer's attention.

Q: *Like what?*

A: Well, if your lawyer thinks that what you are doing might be perfectly legal, but is not in your best interest, the lawyer can share that view with you. Similarly, if your lawyer thinks your planned business decision is misguided . . .

Q: *I go to lawyers for legal advice, not business advice, thank you very much.*

A: Well, you don't have to accept the advice, but lawyers owe clients candid advice about the strengths and weaknesses of their decisions. In fact, some of the best lawyering has occurred when lawyers have advised their clients not to do something stupid.

CHAPTER 5:
YOUR LAWYER MUST BE COMPETENT AND DILIGENT

Q: *How do I know if my lawyer is* **competent**?

A: Lawyers may be **competent** because of special training and experience, or by study and association with other more experienced lawyers. But all legal representation requires some core abilities, which you can ask about.

Q: *You mean the ability to stretch the truth?*

A: No, we mean the ability to know the law, prepare thoroughly, and act promptly to complete the matter. We recommend that you keep these core abilities in mind when you interview prospective lawyers and decide whom to hire.

QUESTIONS TO ASK A LAWYER ABOUT COMPETENCE AND DILIGENCE
1. What kind of experience do you have in handling similar cases?
2. What steps will you take to handle my matter?
3. How will you investigate the facts of the matter?
4. What law is relevant to my case?
5. How will you formulate a legal strategy?
6. What documents will you draft and file? When?
7. Is this a specialized matter? Are you a specialist in such cases?
8. How will we **communicate?**
9. How long will this take you to complete?
10. Are you swamped with work?
11. Where does my matter come in your priorities?

Q: *So, I'm not an expert. How do I know if my lawyer will do a good job?*

A: Nearly every legal representation requires similar steps. Your lawyer will need to *investigate* relevant facts, *understand* relevant law, *formulate* a legal strategy that furthers your goals, and *draft* documents to implement them.

Q: *That sounds great, but the last lawyer I had never returned my phone calls. You call that diligent?*

A: We do not. And, truth be told, the biggest gripe clients have and the most frequent **malpractice** claims are brought against lawyers who fail to return client calls. It is precisely the returning of calls and the prompt attention to your matter that the requirement of diligence is intended to capture. Every lawyer we know has a figurative (or literal) pile of matters that could use a little attention. If yours is among them and a gentle nudge doesn't get you to a priority position, it may be time to think of another lawyer.

CHAPTER 6:
YOUR LAWYER MUST KEEP YOUR CONFIDENCES; OR, MY LIPS ARE SEALED

The lawyer-client relationship is built on trust. Clients must have confidence that their lawyers are in their corner. One aspect of the lawyer rules designed to accomplish this result is what we refer to as the duty of **confidentiality**. This duty requires the lawyer to keep her lips sealed.

Q: *Sealed about what?*

A: In most states a lawyer must keep silent as to all information learned in the course of your representation. This means the lawyer is not free to go to a cocktail party and brag that you are her latest client. It also means a lawyer cannot tell a reporter, a judge or the lawyer on the other side information the lawyer learned in the course of a representation, even if that information could be found by "looking it up" on the internet or down at the local library or courthouse. We say that if the information has not appeared on Action News or in a headline in the Post Gazette then the lawyer must keep quiet about it.

Q: *What is the reason for this rule?*

A: Your lawyer must know the truth—the whole truth—in order to represent you effectively. Sometimes clients are simply reluctant to share their private matters with strangers. Sometimes clients are embarrassed to share the truth. They are ashamed—often needlessly—of what they have done. Sometimes clients think that if they tell their lawyer all of the facts the lawyer will lose enthusiasm for their cause. So, unfortunately, they substitute what they think the lawyer wants to hear for their obligation to tell all.

Not only do lawyers need the whole truth to represent you effectively, but we also know from painful experience that undisclosed facts will come out one way or another. If the truth is known early—and does not make an ill-timed entrance onto the stage—it is much easier to confront head-on and develop a strategy for dealing with it at leisure.

One way to help overcome clients' reluctance to share all facts of their case is for lawyers to look clients in the eye and assure them that the information they are sharing with their lawyer will stay between them and go beyond the privacy of the lawyer-client relationship only with their prior approval. The sanctity of the lawyer-client relationship, we say, is far more important to society than any benefit that would accrue if lawyers did not make this vow of silence to you.

Q: *I know you lawyers; every rule has exceptions, and it seems like you're always talking about some client's case. What are the exceptions here?*

A: Of course, lawyers cannot accomplish anything for clients unless they speak. This reality explains the first exception, which we think you will agree with: Your lawyer can disclose if you consent.

Q: *Why would I do that?*

A: Because you expect your lawyer to accomplish something for you. Say you want your lawyer to negotiate a property sale. You'd want the lawyer to point out the best features about the property so that you can sell it for the best price.

Q: *OK, so I get to say exactly what my lawyer tells the buyer?*

A: Yes and no. In most situations, lawyers rely on your implied authority to disclose information to further your interests. So, your lawyer can proceed without asking you about specifics, but you can limit what your lawyer says by making clear that you do not consent to certain specific disclosures. If the information seems sensitive, your lawyer should ask you about it before disclosing.

Q: *I think I get it. I can control the information flow. But I bet that isn't the only exception.*

A: You are too right there. There has been no more contentious area in the development of the ethics rules for lawyers than whether, and to what extent, lawyers can be permitted, or even required, to disclose client **confidential information** despite our commitment to silence.

The first couple of exceptions are probably not that difficult to accept. If a lawyer knows from client **confidential information** that something will occur that is reasonably likely to result in death or substantial bodily harm, the lawyer is free to disclose that to prevent the untoward results.

Q: *Not required to?*

A: Only a few states require it. The rest leave it to the lawyer's discretion.

Q: *There are more?*

A: Actually, quite a few. The next is that a lawyer can disclose client **confidential information** to defend or assert her own claim.

Q: *That sounds quite self-serving.*

A: You are not the first to make that observation. But if a lawyer gets sued by her client, it could be crippling to her ability to defend herself if she were not able to disclose **confidential information** to do so.

Q: *What about the other direction? Can my lawyer sue me to get her fee?*

A: Yes. The lawyer can use client **confidential information** to help collect a **fee**, but only to the extent absolutely necessary. A lawyer cannot disclose client information unrelated to the matter. If your lawyer knows you are thinking about getting a divorce, she can't disclose that fact in a dispute over how much you owe her for handling the sale of your house. In addition, your lawyer must file any documents that disclose **confidential information** with the court in a way that prevents anyone but the judge and other parties and their lawyers from seeing them.

Q: *What else?*

A: If a lawyer needs to consult another lawyer about some issue arising in a representation, the lawyer may be able to disclose client **confidential information**, but, of course, *that* lawyer must not disclose the information to anyone else.

Q: *Why do I think you've got at least one more?*

A: This is the controversial one. There are a group of exceptions that address the issue of what a lawyer can do when the lawyer learns of a client **fraud**—a deliberate lie to gain an unfair advantage. For example, if a client lies in a court proceeding, her lawyer is required to correct the record.

Q: *What about outside of court?*

A: Well, some states permit lawyers to disclose client **confidential information** to prevent or rectify a client **fraud** outside of court. Most states permit disclosure only if the lawyer's services were used as part of the **fraud**.

Q: *What if that's why the client is consulting the lawyer?*

A: If that happens, it should be clear the lawyer may not disclose any **confidential information**.

Q: *Should?*

A: The exceptions to rectify a client **fraud** don't always make the answer to this question clear. If a client who has been accused of **fraud** seeks out a lawyer, and there is still some way to rectify the consequences of the client's alleged conduct, the lawyer might be free to disclose. But such an exception certainly wouldn't encourage clients to tell lawyers everything.

Q: *Sounds complicated.*

A: It is. The states are all over the place. Some permit disclosure to prevent a **fraud**; others to rectify; still others to prevent or rectify; some require that the lawyer's services be involved; others don't have the requirement. But the truth is lawyers very rarely disclose client **confidential information** in connection with alleged client **fraud**. Indeed, it is safe to say the profession has spent more time debating this issue— with its resulting crazy-quilt set of varying rules—than lawyers have spent actually making such disclosures.

Q: *Is that it?*

A: Well, there is one more. It's only been adopted in a couple states, but it's now a rule recommended by the American Bar Association, so it may get adopted by more. This one relates only to what we call organizational clients—companies, partnerships, associations, not-for-profits.

If a lawyer believes that the highest authority in the organization—its board, its general partner, its trustees—is acting in a way that will bring great harm to the organization, the lawyer is then free to disclose client **confidential information** to prevent that result, but only if she has first brought it to the board's attention.

Q: *Wow! A lawyer can overrule my board of directors?*

A: That's what the rule permits. The board would have to be way out of bounds in the eyes of the lawyer to trigger its provisions but, if that were the case, the lawyer could contact the client's regulators or take other disclosure action to prevent significant harm to the organization.

Q: *I guess I'm glad I'm an individual client. By the way, my lawyer did not describe all of this to me when we started the representation. Does that mean my lawyer does not plan to take advantage of any of these disclosure opportunities?*

A: The truth is most lawyers do not dwell on these matters in conversations with clients. They explain their obligation of **confidentiality** to put clients at ease. They recognize that if they went through what we have discussed here, the benefits of **confidentiality** might disappear.

Clients would view the **confidentiality** requirement as a somewhat hollow promise. But as we observed earlier, "an informed consumer ...."

QUESTIONS TO ASK A LAWYER ABOUT CONFIDENTIALITY
1. Will you keep confidential everything you learn about me or my case?
2. When will you seek my consent to disclose **confidential information**?
3. Do you anticipate that you will be required to disclose anything, such as:
a. To a court, in court papers or other proceedings?
b. To a third party because the law requires certain disclosures?

Q: *That brings up a question: How long does this* **confidentiality** *commitment last?*

A: Forever. Your former lawyer may never voluntarily disclose or use adverse to your interests your **confidential information**. We will talk more abut this obligation when we address client **loyalty**. And there is one more thing.

Q: *Uh oh!*

A: This is important. **Confidentiality** means the lawyer may not *voluntarily* disclose any of this information. As we said, no locker room or cocktail party chatter. But if the lawyer is ever required to testify in a proceeding, a different set of rules applies.

Q: *More bad news?*

A: You could say that. Your lawyer would be forced to testify as to all information learned in the course of the representation unless the subject matter comes within the attorney-client privilege.

Q: *What's the privilege?*

A: It says that the lawyer cannot be forced to testify about confidential conversations between client and lawyer for purposes of receiving legal advice. For example, if you talk to your lawyer about your golf game, unless you are Tiger Woods, the conversation is not privileged because your dismal scores have nothing to do with legal advice. If you talk about your plans for building a shopping center or how you are worried that you might be convicted of reckless driving, your lawyer cannot be forced to recount those conversations ever—even after you've gone to your heavenly reward—because those are conversations seeking legal advice. Your golf scores are "confidential" (because your lawyer learned them from you) but they aren't privileged (because they are irrelevant to why you went to see the lawyer). Your fears and hopes for the representation are both confidential and privileged. If you think of all **confidential information** as coming within a giant circle, then the privileged information—about which the lawyer may not be forced to testify—is a smaller circle wholly within the larger one.

Q: *So the privilege applies only in court?*

A: Yes, that's correct. There are some specific requirements that must be met before the privilege will apply, and it is your lawyer's job to see that it is done. For example, only conversations between client and lawyer with no third-party witnesses can be certain to meet that requirement. So if you are the client and you bring your son or your accountant with you to meet your lawyer and your lawyer asks them to step outside, don't be offended. Your lawyer is only taking the appropriate precautions to make sure your conversations stay protected. Long after your representation ends, your lawyer is required to assert the privilege and notify you that she has been called to testify so that you can assert the privilege in whatever form is appropriate.

"I never discuss my clients with their mothers."

CHAPTER 7:
YOUR LAWYER MUST BE LOYAL

Another core value of the client-lawyer relationship is your lawyer's commitment to be loyal to you. A client is entitled to rely on the fact that her lawyer will not be limited by commitments to others that would compromise her lawyer's ardor.

CONFLICTS OF INTEREST

Q: *Loyalty sounds good but what's the reality? I just know you've got more exceptions.*

A: Actually, I haven't. The first obligation of your lawyer in this regard is to search his heart and his database to make sure there are no conflicts.

Q: *What an odd combination.*

A: Not really. Your lawyer's **loyalty** obligation begins with a search for those conflicts that might get in the way of total **loyalty**. In fact, your lawyer has several different duties that are designed to make him more effective by being independent to represent you.

Q: *You'll excuse me if I don't applaud quite yet.*

A: Fair enough. One way your lawyer must be independent is that he has to assure you there are no other loyalties he has to others that will interfere with his ability to represent you effectively. Your lawyer's representation of you has to be independent of your lawyer's and your lawyer's **law firm**'s **loyalty** to other clients, third parties or his own self-interest.

Q: *I like that kind of independence. There's more?*

A: You'll like this one, too. As we discussed elsewhere, your lawyer has to maintain his independence from any third party who is paying his **fees**, whether it is the client's dad, employer or insurance company. So, if your lawyer has some personal reason why the representation might be fettered—he has a prejudice or a business interest that might materially reduce his ardor—that interest must be disclosed to you. Similarly, if your lawyer or any other lawyer in his practice—even if he is in a 1,000-person **law firm**—represents your adversary, your lawyer must first ask whether a **reasonable** lawyer could conclude that the other representation would not significantly interfere with representing you and, even if he so concludes, he must then (a) tell you about the matter, and (b) let you decide, after being fully informed of the circumstances, whether you will permit the representation to proceed nonetheless.

Q: *Meaning, can I live with it?*

A: Exactly. It's entirely your decision. Does it bother you that someone else in the firm is doing work for your adversary? That's the question you must ask. At the same time your lawyer will have to tell the **law firm**'s other client about the possible representation of you and determine if that client will consent to his firm representing you.

Q: *My lawyer's going to tell my adversary about my request for services?*

A: Great question. You have learned your **confidentiality** lessons well. Your lawyer may seek permission from your adversary to proceed with your representation only if you agree that he may contact this other client. If you give your lawyer permission, he can make the call; if not, the call does not get made and your search for a lawyer continues.

Q: *Doesn't sound like a real choice. If I decide to go elsewhere, the law firm, since I didn't hire them, will now tell the other side, right?*

A: Wrong. One measure of the **loyalty** of lawyers is that we owe **loyalty** obligations even to folks who never hire us. Anyone who calls a lawyer is a prospective client. And lawyers are forbidden from ever disclosing the **confidential information** of prospective clients in exactly the same way they must protect **confidential information** of current and former clients.

In addition, if lawyers learn **confidential information** from prospective clients, the fact that they know that information may prevent them from taking on other representations adverse to that client.

Q: *Why? What's the catch?*

A: No catch at all. As long as the **confidential information** was learned in the same or substantially related legal matter, the lawyer (and the lawyer's firm) is barred from taking on any subsequent adverse representation.

Oh, there is one catch.

Q: *I knew there was! What is it?*

A: There is a new rule that a few states have adopted. That rule allows a **law firm** to take on a matter where **confidential information** from a prospective client might otherwise preclude the new representation—if two conditions are met.

Q: *I'll bet one condition is the size of the fee …*

A: Don't be so cynical. One is that the lawyer didn't learn too much.

Q: *And the other?*

A: The lawyer or lawyers who learned the information are screened from the new matter.

Q: *Screened?*

A: That's something we'll discuss in just a moment.

Q: *It all sounds so complicated.*

A: It's not, really. But for firms of many lawyers to maintain, in an accessible form, all of the data on past and present clients is quite demanding. You can see, however, how this will protect you once you become a client. Should any lawyer in your lawyer's **law firm** ever consider representing anyone in a matter directly adverse to you, before the firm can take that matter on, the **law firm** must notify you of the nature of the matter, regardless of whether it is related to the representation the firm is handling for you, and must receive your consent to the **law firm**'s proposed new representation.

Q: *A powerful veto.*

A: Exactly. But the rule reflects the profession's commitment to client **loyalty** and, despite the complaints of many lawyers who hate to send new business out the door, the profession has essentially held the line on this important principle.

Q: *Essentially? I knew there were some exceptions here as well.*

A: I have to admit you are correct. But they are quite narrow.

The first is irrelevant to you, unless you are a government. Because the profession wants to encourage lawyers to work in the public service and not make it too difficult for those dedicated lawyers to re-enter the private sector, a **law firm** may hire a former government lawyer—without creating a **conflict of interest**—even if that lawyer was adverse to a present or future client of the firm. The government lawyer must be screened from the matter, but the government is stuck with the fact that its lawyer now works at the **law firm** on the other side.

Q: *Screened? That's the second time you've mentioned that word.*

A: I know. It's a funny word. You probably think of a screen as what you put in your windows in the spring to let in light, sound and air, while keeping out mosquitoes. But in ethics parlance a screen refers to the process of blocking the lawyer with the conflict entirely from getting involved in the matter he previously handled. The lawyers handling the matter cannot have any conversations regarding it with the former government lawyer.

Screens are put in place all the time when clients are asked to permit a lawyer to take on an otherwise conflicting matter. The client can say no; the client can say yes; or the client can give instructions on how the screen must be implemented.

But what we are talking about here is involuntary screening where the client is simply told the conflict issue has been "solved" by a screen.

Q: *How does the government know its former lawyer is behaving behind that screen?*

A: It doesn't. It simply must trust its former lawyer because all of the compliance (or non-compliance) takes place in the lawyer's new practice setting, which is why the idea of screens has been so controversial.

Q: *Is that the only exception?*

A: I am afraid not. A few states have given the same right to private lawyers who switch from one firm to the other. If they are screened, these lawyers, in effect, can switch sides without disqualifying their new firm.

Q: *And these screens are the only protection?*

A: Exactly; the side-switching lawyer may not participate in the matter. And the client has no way of monitoring the effectiveness of the screen. It can cause justifiable anxiety in clients. The good news is that very rarely has a screen been breached.

Q: *How would one know?*

A: That's certainly a good question but anecdotally the situations where it has come to light are few and far between.

Q: *Are we done with chinks in your loyalty commitment?*

A: Now, now. We would call these slight scratches. But there is one more. Some **law firms** have taken to rewriting our profession's rules in their engagement agreements. They inform their clients typically as follows:

> We also wish to emphasize that [**law firm**] provides a wide array of legal services to many clients around the world. We therefore ask each of our clients to agree that we may continue to represent or may undertake in the future to represent existing or new clients in any matter that is not substantially related to our work for you, even if the interests of such clients in those unrelated matters are directly adverse to yours.

What they are saying is that without asking your permission they can take a position directly adverse to you so long as it is on a matter unrelated to your representation.

Q: *Can they do that?*

A: That's unclear at the moment. Some argue that such an arrangement should only work if the client is extremely knowledgeable. Others argue that no client should be asked to provide such a prospective **waiver** of a future **conflict of interest**, no matter how knowledgeable.

Q: *They don't know what they're waiving, right?*

A: That's precisely one key point. When the client grants such a **waiver**, the client has no idea what the matter will be as to which the client has theoretically given a **waiver**. Nor will the client know the timing of the conflicting representation. The other key point is that at the time of the **waiver** the client has no idea what kind of representations the lawyer will undertake for the client between the date the letter is signed and the date the lawyer undertakes the "waived" conflict. The client also doesn't know what **confidential information** will have been shared with the lawyer over the months or years between signing and the adverse representation.

Q: *My solution would be to just fire the lawyer. Won't that solve the problem?*

A: Well, the first solution is to refuse to agree to the prospective **waiver**. But for those who are misled into signing them, one solution is to assert that the **waiver** is invalid. That argument might succeed. Or you could fire the lawyer. The problem with the latter is that your wish to fire your lawyer may arise at exactly the time when it would be very inconvenient to be forced to find new counsel. While clients have the absolute right to fire their lawyers at any time for any reason or no reason at all, if the lawyer is about to go to trial or in the middle of a major transaction, the remedy of firing one's lawyer can be self-defeating. More important, no client should have to injure himself in order to secure the **loyalty** to which he is entitled.

Q: *If clients can fire their lawyers, can lawyers fire their clients? That would be one way around all this **loyalty** stuff.*

A: True enough. Lawyers are entitled to **withdraw** from a representation for no reason at all, so long as the **withdrawal** does not have a material adverse affect on the client. But one thing lawyers may not do is fire a client to make it possible to take on a new client. We are saddened to tell you some lawyers have tried that ploy; but the courts have dealt with them harshly.

Q: *Are we done?*

A: I think so. I also don't want you to get the wrong impression. Though we spent far longer discussing the exceptions to the **loyalty** lawyers owe present clients than we did discussing the basic **loyalty** principle, the fact is 99% of all representations, and maybe a higher percentage, reflect adherence to the basic principles. Quite simply, lawyers turn down hundreds of matters every day because they would involve taking a position adverse to a present or former client of their firm.

QUESTIONS TO ASK A LAWYER ABOUT CONFLICTS OF INTEREST

1. Have you done a **conflicts check** in your **law firm** to see whether you can take my case?
2. Has that check disclosed:
   a. Any personal conflicts of **law firm** lawyers which could influence my representation?
   b. Any current clients of the **law firm** whose interests could influence my representation?
   c. Any former clients of the **law firm** whose interests could influence my representation?
3. If yes, what are those interests, and do you reasonably believe you can proceed in my representation?

SPECIFIC PROBLEMATIC CONFLICTS

There is also a series of special rules that govern how a lawyer conducts a representation, all designed to enhance the lawyer's **loyalty**.

Q: *So many rules!*

A: For your benefit.

1. Doing Business with Your Lawyer

If a lawyer is to do business with a client beyond the legal representation, he must do three things: a) have the client consent to the arrangement in writing; b) assure that the transaction is entirely fair; and c) advise the client of the benefits to the client of being separately represented in the matter. This means that when a lawyer does business with his own client, the transaction will be scrutinized for compliance with these particular requirements and will always be subject to second-guessing on the fairness question.

The rule has quite a broad reach. For example, if a lawyer agrees to take his **fee** in shares of the client's company, that part of the engagement qualifies as doing business with a client, and therefore must comply with these special rules and can be subject to the second-guessing discussed above.

Q: *So if I find a lawyer to work for shares in my company, I might get out of giving him the shares?*

A: You certainly could try, if your lawyer didn't cross every "t" and dot every "i."

2. Giving Your Lawyer a Gift

Q: *Not that I would, but I can't leave my lawyer money in my will?*

A: That's correct; unless you hire a different lawyer in a different firm to write it. Or the person making the gift is a relative of the lawyer. But a lawyer (and the lawyer's firm colleagues) may not prepare any document in which a client makes a gift—now or in the future—to his lawyer. That way, the profession saves lawyers from lots of claims of over-reaching when a client dies and leaves the bulk of her estate to "her loving lawyer."

3. No Movie Rights

Q: *Maybe I can save fees this way. Instead of paying my lawyer, I'll give him the TV rights to my fascinating story.*

A: Putting a great crimp in the ambitions of every lawyer who secretly dreams of being a Hollywood mogul, there is a rule that prohibits a lawyer from negotiating for the book or film rights to a client's story until after the representation has terminated. We don't want lawyers having a keener interest in the client's matter being covered on *60 Minutes* than they have in the best interests of the client.

4. No Subsidizing Clients

Q: *I'm broke. The accident has wiped me out and the other guy's insurance company knows it. Can my lawyer help with my rent until we settle?*

A: This rule has often been questioned but remains intact: The only financial assistance a lawyer may provide the non-indigent client is the *advancing* of the cost and **expenses** of **litigation**; as to those who are indigent, the lawyer may pay (without any agreement for repayment) for those same items. Thus, lawyers confronted with desperate clients who need money now may not fortify their clients to resist an early low ball offer from defendants who wish to take advantage of those circumstances by agreeing to help the client with living **expenses** until the case can be tried or a more realistic settlement offer is secured.

The theory behind the rule is that by prohibiting such assistance the lawyer does not gain too great an interest in the outcome of the matter; in a world in which **contingent fees** are already in the one-third to 40% range, it is hard to imagine how the extra interest arising from help with living **expenses** would make a difference. But for the present that is the rule, except in a few places, like California and the District of Columbia, where lawyers are allowed to provide financial assistance to clients, but only if necessary to maintain the legal action.

5. No Buying Client Claims

Q: *If he can't pay my rent, maybe I'll sell him another 25% of my claim.*

A: A lawyer is also prohibited from acquiring any interest in a **litigation** matter that the lawyer is handling other than the lawyer's interest in a **fee**. The lawyer may not, for example, purchase 25% of the client's claim. As a result, the financially strapped client will have to look beyond his lawyer if he is in desperate need of funds for sustaining the **litigation** or any other purpose.

6. Lawyers as Directors

The arena of client **loyalty** is very broad. For example, we have special considerations if the lawyer is asked to go on the board of directors of a client.

Q: *Sounds like a great business generating plan.*

A: That can be one of the pluses and one of the minuses. Being in the board room certainly reduces the chances that the client will look elsewhere for services. But if anyone wants to challenge the use of the

law firm, the idea that the lawyer/director steered work to the **law firm** might be viewed skeptically.

Q: *Any other problems with it?*

A: Absolutely. If a lawyer/director is giving advice to the board, will these conversations be considered privileged? Was the lawyer/director talking as a lawyer or as a director when he spoke out on the issue?

In addition, if the client gets sued relating to a matter that came before the board, the company may lose the services of its longtime **law firm** because the **litigation** creates a **conflict of interest** between client and lawyer, something that might not have occurred if the lawyer had only worn one hat.

7. Coercive Settlements

Here's another way lawyers must remain independent. Say you had a lawsuit against a car company. You bought a lemon. The car company said it would pay you an extra $10,000 if your lawyer agreed never to sue the car company again.

Q: *Great!*

A: Great for you, but not for your lawyer; and not for all those like you who want to draw on a lawyer's expertise in suing the car company. So we have a rule that says a lawyer may not offer or accept a settlement that restricts his right to practice law in the future, even if the extra money is offered to the lawyer.

Q: *To the lawyer! I hope not.*

A: You are right there. The rule really assures that the lawyer on the other side won't put your lawyer in an awkward position.

8. Sexual Relationships with Clients

The last rule is an absolute: A lawyer cannot engage in a sexual relationship with a client, unless that relationship predated the client-lawyer representation.

Q: *Never? What if I'm single and attracted to my lawyer?*

A: Then your lawyer has to decide whether to represent you or date you. Another lawyer in the **law firm** can take over your representation.

The rule is absolute to prevent a lawyer's even unintentional use of trust in the client-lawyer relationship for the lawyer's own advantage or the client's disadvantage.

FORMER LAWYERS

Q: *What about after the representation is over? What **loyalty** do I get then? I sure don't want my former lawyer turning on me.*

A: Well, you get significant but nonetheless limited comfort in that regard. The day after a representation ends, a lawyer can take on a matter directly adverse to the brand new "former client," unless the new representation is substantially related to the prior matter.

Q: *Sounds like one of those large lawyer loopholes to me.*

A: Not really. It's actually a rule designed to protect clients, without making the client's former lawyer bound to his former client forever. The real purpose here is to protect the former client's **confidential information** learned in the earlier representation. But if the former client objects to what his former lawyer is doing, we don't want the client to be forced to disclose the **confidential information** he shared with his former lawyer in order to protect it. So all the client needs to demonstrate is the relationship between what the lawyer did for the client in the past and the new matter the lawyer is now handling.

Q: *Can you give me an example?*

A: Suppose I represented you in getting zoning for a shopping center. Now some shopkeeper wants me to represent him in leasing space from you in the same center. On the surface it looks like the matters might be substantially related. But in fact, the two matters involve such different questions that, unless it turns out I learned from you **confidential information** on your leasing plans while I was helping you get the zoning, I should be able to take the matter on.

In contrast, what if I were asked to represent a group that wanted to challenge the proposed shopping center because it's in a flood plain? Even if when you and I were doing the zoning, the word "environmental" did not cross our lips, I would still be prohibited from representing the environmentalists.

Q: *Why?*

A: Because, even if the two representations are factually and legally distinct, I would be fouling the nest, or attacking the fruits of the very same legal services I provided to you in the first place. While representing someone who wants to rent in your shopping center furthers your purposes, representing this do-good green crowd would undermine the very project for which I was paid to give you assistance.

Q: *Is that the end of the lawyer's **loyalty** obligations?*

A: No, not at all. There are special rules that govern situations when you're not paying your lawyer.

Q: *I like saving money ... but I do want a loyal lawyer.*

LAWYERS SELECTED OR PAID FOR BY OTHERS

One of the most important principles of client **loyalty** is one of the hardest for lawyers to fulfill. No matter who is writing the checks, the lawyer must remain independent of his benefactor and committed to the client.

Q: *So say I hire a lawyer to represent my son in a minor run-in with the police. I'm of course interested in the representation and call them for information about how it's going.*

A: Any information you ask for must be met with a polite but firm response that this information about your son is confidential.

Q: *I don't like that response. How do your rules protect me?*

A: Think about how this issue plays out much more frequently—in the situation where an insurance company hires a lawyer to represent you, the insured, say in an automobile accident case. Sometimes the insured won't really care. You just want the insurance company to take care of the messy situation. That's why you bought insurance. Under these circumstances, even though you, the insured, are the technical client, the lawyer can take his marching orders from the insurance company, which in some states is considered a co-client but in others is not.

But there are many cases in which the interests of the insured are at odds with the insurance company. It might be because the claim is greater than the amount of insurance; it might be because the insurance company has written a letter "reserving its rights," that it is not agreeing that some or all of the claim is covered by insurance; it might be because the insured has reputational interest in the case and might not want the insurance company to settle because of some non-monetary concerns. Whatever the issue, it creates a real **conflict of interest** between the insurance company and the insured.

For example, the insurance company may claim the matter is resolved by some clause in the insurance contract.

Q: *Who ever reads those?*

A: Exactly. Moreover, a lawyer's ethical obligations today cannot be changed through the use of a form contract in six-point type someone threw in a drawer years ago. Anyway, in those situations, the lawyer must remember that his **loyalty** is to the insured.

Q: *Even though he gets paid by the insurance company?*

A: And that's the rub. Typically, insurance companies will hire **law firms** to handle hundreds of these cases. The insurance company, of course, is the source of the funding. And although the insured is assigned to this **law firm** for this one matter, the insured is unlikely to use the **law firm**'s services ever again. You can sense the tension that inevitably arises. Nonetheless, the lawyer must be loyal to the insured, though there is one limit. The lawyer hired by the insurance company to defend the insured will not represent either party if they should come to blows. But the lawyer may never share with the insurance company **confidential information** learned from the client that might hurt the insured in any dispute with the insurance company.

SHARING A LAWYER

Another aspect of lawyer **loyalty** is how the lawyer handles joint representations.

Q: *Like buyers and sellers of real estate?*

A: That's one example. It is possible in certain situations for one lawyer to represent multiple parties who are on opposite sides of a transaction. Some refer to this as lawyer for the situation.

Q: *You lawyers must hate that, cutting down on the number of lawyers needed.*

A: We do, but not necessarily for that reason. The issue to be decided is whether the parties who come to the lawyer, like buyer and seller, have truly decided everything they need to determine in order to go forward with the transaction.

Say they want to transfer real estate. And they've decided on price, date of settlement, and the description of the property. As they sit before the lawyer, the lawyer realizes they haven't discussed a termite clause. If he is representing both of them, what does he do? It's in the interest of the buyer to have one; it's in the interest of the seller not to. But if, in fact, sophisticated parties really have reached agreement on everything important, it is possible for a lawyer to represent both.

When I was talking about joint representations, I had in mind clients who appear to have the same interest as they show up in the lawyer's office. Think of three women who want to start a business.

Q: *They don't want to have to hire three lawyers.*

A: For sure. And they want to go into business together and have a huge success. But let's assume one will put up the money, the second has the idea and the third will work full-time in the business. You can see how their interests might not be the same. The money person wants a big return on his investment. The worker would like a big salary. Maybe the idea person wants to be able to sell the idea to others or get a royalty for the idea. And these are the conflicts they presently have before there might be any falling out among them over the progress the business is making. A lawyer may represent each person in this group. But before he does, he must remind each how getting his own lawyer might be a better idea as well as explain the limitations on his representation if they will all be his clients.

"If it pleases the Court, Your Honor, I'd like to quit the defense and join the prosecution."

CHAPTER 8:
WHAT TO DO IF SOMETHING
GOES WRONG

Q: *I am an unhappy camper. At $150 an hour my lawyer should be delivering better services than I'm receiving.*

A: We are human. That means we strive for perfection in all our relationships but rarely succeed in achieving that goal. Your relationship with your lawyer is not any different. Lawyer and client should strive for bliss but when that is not the result, it is critical that the problems not be allowed to fester. As painful as it might be, they should be addressed.

TALK TO YOUR LAWYER

In this part of the book, we have emphasized that you are entitled to an awful lot from your lawyer. And your lawyer is entitled to a fair amount from you. Each might disappoint the other. The key for you—our worthy client—is not to stew in silence, longing for a phone call from your busy advocate, resenting writing checks, uncertain your matter is receiving the attention it deserves.

Q: *Why should I have to start the conversation?*

A: Remember, you are in charge. Discuss your concerns with your lawyer. We know it can be uncomfortable, that it takes guts to raise an unpleasant topic, and we know that lawyers often avoid these uncomfortable conversations as well. But long before matters get out of hand, long before the mention of your lawyer's name makes you cringe, you should muster the courage to bring up your concerns. And if you don't think you can do it face to face or over the telephone, write a letter or e-mail, or, if your lawyer works at a firm, contact someone else at that firm to explain your feelings and start the search for a solution. You will be pleasantly surprised at how anxious your lawyer's firm will be to address your issues and turn you into a happy client. We can assure you the least expensive solution to being an unhappy client is talking to your lawyer or your lawyer's colleagues.

QUESTIONS TO ASK IF SOMETHING GOES WRONG
1. Will you please tell me about_____?
2. Have you made a mistake that will affect my case?
3. Why won't you do what I ask? (See sidebar Chapter 9).
4. Why does your fee differ from what I expected? (See sidebar Chapter 3)
5. What are my alternatives in this situation?
6. What steps will you take to remedy this situation?
7. When will you take this action?
8. Should I speak to your **law firm** colleagues about this?
9. Whom should I speak to?
10. Have other clients ever expressed the same concern?
11. What happens if I decide to find another lawyer?

PUT IT IN WRITING

Q: *And if that doesn't work?*
A: If conversation does not bring a cure, and you remain unhappy, a more formal approach may be in order. If you have not done so already, write your lawyer, explaining your complaints, documenting them as best you can. Be particular: Describe each instance or respect in which you believe your lawyer has let you down.

This further step has three benefits. First, it will clarify your thinking and force you to consider whether your gripes are really that serious. Second, it might get your lawyer's attention in the way a phone call did not. Sometimes people only hear what they want to hear. But a clear writing is hard to ignore. Third, the documentation will provide you with "proof" of your **communication** should you later wish to assert that your lawyer is not entitled to **fees** either already paid or now being sought and, worse comes to worse, if you should ever assert a claim against your lawyer for failing to fulfill his obligations to you.

END THE RELATIONSHIP

Q: *I've had the conversation and I'm still unhappy. Now what?*

A: While as with any relationship, problems should be addressed rather than ignored, and parting company should be a last, not a first, resort; you are in fact free to fire your lawyer at any time for any reason or no reason at all. But such a choice is not necessarily cost-free. First, the firing of the lawyer does not relieve you of the obligation to pay **fees** for all unbilled time plus any outstanding invoices. In the case in which the lawyer was retained on a **contingent fee**, if you are ultimately successful being represented by successor counsel, you will be responsible to pay your first lawyer what is called **quantum meruit**, a Latin term for the amount the first lawyer deserves for the contribution the first lawyer made to the overall result. This sum is often measured simply by the number of hours the lawyer dedicated to the matter times a **reasonable** hourly rate, but it can also be calculated based on the value of the contribution, a number you might argue should be zero or very little because of your dissatisfaction with your initial counsel. In any event, when hiring a successor lawyer on a **contingent fee**, you must make arrangements that take into account the **fee** owed the fired lawyer. You don't want to owe two **fees**! Your new lawyer may be able to help you with this negotiation.

Besides the **fee** obligation, you must consider the slippage that will occur in the handling of your matter as the new counsel gets up to speed as well as the need to compensate the first counsel for any time the predecessor spends assisting with that process. There also is the fact that replacing counsel is a highly public event. While there may be no basis for doing so, the party on the other side will invariably take some comfort, if not delight, in seeing your decision to switch lawyers as a sign of weakness or dissension.

All that having been said, sometimes divorce is the only choice. But it has to be the last choice.

CONTACT THE DISCIPLINARY AUTHORITY

Q: *This lawyer's so bad, I want to make sure he doesn't end up lying to and abandoning other clients like he did me. But everyone tells me your lawyer discipline system just brushes everything under the rug. Not surprising since it's run by lawyers.*

A: No, the truth is that lawyers can get in lots of trouble for violating the rules we discuss in this book. Anyone with a complaint about a lawyer can file a complaint with your state disciplinary authority.

Here's what to do: Contact your local or state bar association and find out how to file such a complaint. Many staff in these offices will talk to you informally before you decide to take any action.

Q: *That sounds intimidating.*

A: Not really. All it takes is a letter describing for the disciplinary folks the conduct of the lawyer. The more detail, the better. Filing a. complaint doesn't mean the lawyer will be disciplined, but it does mean your complaint will be reviewed.

Q: *So, if my lawyer doesn't return my phone calls, I get to file a complaint?*

A: Well, that's a bit drastic for the first time that happens. But if it happens repeatedly, that is precisely what you can do.

Q: *What do you mean by discipline?*

A: The sanctions that can be imposed on a lawyer range from a private reprimand all the way up to total disbarment, depending on the seriousness of the offense.

Q: *I guess you lawyers probably have a whole lot of private reprimands.*

A: There are many, but that doesn't mean that sanction is so minor. You would be surprised how upset lawyers get when any sanction is threatened and how seriously they try to avoid even the "minor" sanction of a private reprimand. For the rest of their lives they may be forced to disclose that fact each time they seek to appear in a different court or apply to join the bar of a different state.

Q: *I guess you've got it set up so the public never finds out about this.*

A: Not true at all. In some states even the initial complaints are public. In almost all states if the disciplinary authorities decide to proceed against the lawyer, the proceeding becomes public, and all discipline against lawyers except private reprimands are public and sent to a national data bank.

SEEK LEGAL RELIEF

1. Malpractice

Q: *Sounds like getting a lawyer in trouble with the Bar won't put any money in my pocket; might even hurt my chances of getting what I deserve. I would rather make the lawyer pay me for his mistakes than deal with the disciplinary people.*

A: You can do that too. In addition to discipline, lawyers can be sued for breaching their fiduciary duties to you and for breaching the standard of care they owe you. If you can prove you were damaged by the lawyer's misconduct, you can collect damages. And even if you can't prove damages, you may be able to force the lawyer to return some or all of the **fee** because of the misconduct.

Q: *Yeah. I guess that requires me to have another uncaring lawyer.*

A: You are right there. To file a disciplinary complaint, no lawyer is required. But **if** you think you have a claim against your lawyer for money damages, you will be well served to have a lawyer to press your claim. In fact you may have to hire two lawyers.

Q: *Two lawyers! Where will it end?*

A: We don't mean to scare you, but bringing a **malpractice** claim against a lawyer without having one yourself is a recipe for failure. And in order to prove a **malpractice** claim you will need to have an expert witness—another lawyer—to testify that your former lawyer's conduct failed to meet the standard of care lawyers owe their clients.

2. Fee Forfeiture

Q: *My lawyer represented me in a case. Now I find out—after the fact and quite by accident—that the whole time my lawyer's firm was representing the other side on a different matter. They didn't tell me. I'm not sure I've been injured. We did pretty well. But the **law firm** took a big contingent fee and I feel betrayed.*

A: Even if you weren't hurt financially, you might have a remedy. Lawyers with undisclosed conflicts often can be forced to give back or disgorge the **fee** they received on the ground that the **breach of fiduciary duty** should not go unrectified and that lawyers with such divided loyalties did not "earn" the **fee** they received.

Q: *Sounds great. How do I get my money back?*

A: As with **malpractice** suits, you will have to hire another lawyer to sue for it. This time you won't have to prove you were harmed, but you will have to point out the specific **fiduciary duty** your lawyer breached.

3. Disqualification

Q: *What if I had learned about this other representation during the case? What could I have done then?*

A: You could have done two things. You could have filed a motion to remove your **law firm** from handling the *other* matter. Lawyers are regularly disqualified, as we call it, from representing clients when they are operating under a conflict that that has not been properly responded to. You could also fire the lawyer and demand a return of any **fees** you previously paid the lawyer on the matter. Actually, you could do both; that depends on whether you want the lawyer to continue to help you.

"My incompetence will become the basis of your appeal."

PART THREE

WHAT NOT TO EXPECT FROM YOUR LAWYER

CHAPTER 9:
YOU AND YOUR LAWYER MUST OBEY
THE LAW

Your lawyer is your advocate, she is in your corner, she is ready to go to bat for you and only you. Pick your favorite metaphor. Any of them will help you understand what heroes we want to be on your behalf.

Q: *That's probably why everyone hates lawyers—except their own.*

A: Yes, we have often said that if lawyers were winning popularity contests then we wouldn't be doing our jobs. But while we are breaking our arms patting ourselves on the back about how wonderful we are, we need to throw some cautionary words your way. There are limits. Places lawyers should not (and, we hope, will not) go.

QUESTIONS TO ASK A LAWYER WHO WILL NOT DO WHAT YOU EXPECT

1. Why won't you do what I request?
2. Are you afraid that my request will violate a lawyer code provision?
   a. If so, which one?
   b. Have you sought advice about whether this is a clear violation?
3. Are you afraid that my request might violate some other law?
   a. If so, which one?
      i. If my request is a crime, which one and why?
      ii. If my request is a **fraud**, why?
      iii. If my request would violate some court rules or procedures, which ones and why?
      iv. If my request would require you or me to violate some other legal provision, which one and why?
   b. If not, or if you cannot tell me which law, then why are you afraid to proceed?

Q: *I don't want you pulling any punches*.

A: Well there are some punches lawyers may not land. Let us give you some examples.

YOUR LAWYER CANNOT VIOLATE THE RULES OF PROFESSIONAL CONDUCT

First, a lawyer may not violate the **rules of professional conduct**. So if you ask your long-time lawyer to negotiate a loan for you from Big Bank, and someone else in the lawyer's firm is representing Big Bank on some totally unrelated matter, unless Big Bank and you both waive the **conflict of interest**, your lawyer may not take that matter on. The same would be true if the other side offered you an extra $100,000 if your lawyer agreed never to take a case on against the other side. The condition on that payment, if accepted, violates our rules. So even though it would be in your interest for the lawyer to do that, the obligation of the lawyer not to violate the rules trumps the lawyer's agreeing to something that would certainly be in your best interest.

YOUR LAWYER CANNOT COMMIT CRIMES, OR HELP YOU COMMIT CRIMES

Second, lawyers—just like clients—cannot violate the criminal law. Every once in a while lawyers find themselves, in connection with client matters, being asked to assist a client plan or program that would result in the lawyer aiding and abetting a client violation of law.

Q: *Most crimes are obvious. I wouldn't do that.*

A: Many are. But more and more areas of life are now subject to criminal regulation, from environmental protections to leashing your dog.

Q: *Can you explain?*

A: Certainly. Say you are active politically. You want to help a candidate for Congress. But you and your family already gave the campaign finance limit. So you go to your lawyers and ask them to help this congressional candidate. So far, so good. You are certainly allowed to encourage others to help your guy. But then, if you tell your lawyers they can add the amount of their contributions to your next invoice, you have crossed the line. And so have your lawyers, if they comply with your suggestion. If they contribute money, that is fine. When they charge their contributions back to you "for professional services," they have aided and abetted a campaign finance law violation and maybe much more.

FRAUD: YOUR LAWYER CANNOT LIE, OR HELP YOU LIE

Lawyers also may not make misrepresentations or otherwise act in a dishonest manner. A lawyer's word is supposed to be her bond.

Q: *Sounds like an absurd idea. You are always trying to get people off even when you know they are guilty. This tells me that lawyers and truth part company on a regular basis.*

A: Hardly. But we take your point. Lawyers as advocates do assert propositions they might not, in their hearts, believe to be correct. But they only do so in situations where they have a good faith basis for making the assertion. We'll give you an example. Suppose you have a contract dispute, and you claim the other side promised to pay you a bonus of $10,000 if you sold a certain number of storm windows. The other side insists it never made that promise. Even if your lawyer in her heart thinks your claim is shaky, the lawyer may argue that you are entitled to a bonus—unless the lawyer knows you are lying.

Q: *Guess it doesn't pay for you lawyers to know, am I right?*

A: Lawyers would prefer to know the truth. But the truth may in fact be unknown. People have honest misunderstandings all the time. Memories fade. Ambiguous language is used. People change their minds. It is for judges and juries—not lawyers—to determine the truth. It is for lawyers to advocate without lying or making misrepresentations.

Q: *That is what you were talking about?*

A: Correct. Though that was an important digression. But let us give you a few concrete examples. Say you want to determine whether a certain food company is selling fresh meat. You think the only way to do that is to gain access to the company's facility. So you ask your lawyer to send one of her **paralegals** into the plant posing as a fire safety inspector from an insurance company.

Q: *Clever idea.*

A: Too clever by half. A lawyer cannot misrepresent who she is. And another rule says a lawyer cannot do through the acts of another what she can't do herself. So the **paralegal** cannot be sent in.

Or, you're in negotiations. The other side wants to know how the property's zoned. The lawyer calls you to check, and you say, "Tell them it's zoned commercial." The lawyer asks, "It is?" And you respond, "No. But that will entice them into being interested." The lawyer may not pass that information on.

Q: *Wait a minute. What if I tell the lawyer I'll take a million. Then I tell the lawyer to open negotiations by insisting on two. The lawyer's not going to do that?*

A: No. That is different. While lawyers cannot lie, they are free to engage in what we call "puffing." Everyone knows that when a lawyer says "my client won't take a dollar less than $2,000,000," all the lawyer is doing is puffing. But that haggling over price is quite different from telling the other side there are no environmental problems when, in fact, there are buried arsenic tanks out behind the tool shed.

Another limit on lawyer conduct arises when the client lies.

Q: *You mean when the lawyer knows the client lies?*

A: Correct. Actually, the rules have a split. It is one thing when the lawyer knows the client lies. It is another when the lawyer reasonably believes that to be the case. Let's take them one at a time.

If a client lies in connection with negotiations, then the lawyer has to decide whether he is aiding and abetting the client **fraud** by remaining silent. Say it's a big negotiating session and the other side asks a question. The client answers, with an answer the lawyer knows is a lie. Can the lawyer leave the lie uncorrected? That depends on whether the question sought material information and whether the failure to correct the record amounts to **fraud**. But first there is a good lawyering point.

Q: *What's that?*

A: Regardless of whether the lie amounts to **fraud**, the lawyer ought to take the client aside and urge a correction. This is done simply because no one knows what mischief that lie can create later when, with the benefit of hindsight, the other side, unhappy with the "deal," argues that the lie was part of a massive **fraud**.

But assuming the client refuses to correct, the lawyer a) may **withdraw** from the representation; b) must disclose to prevent harm to the other side if the lawyer thinks the lie amounts to **fraud**; and c) may not incorporate the lie into any agreement or other documents the lawyer prepares.

Q: *You said something about "reasonably believes?"*

A: Right. Thanks for the reminder. If a lawyer reasonably believes the client has lied about a material matter, that gives rise to permission (but not a requirement) for her to **withdraw**.

Q: *When else may a lawyer* **withdraw?**

A: Your lawyer must **withdraw** in three different circumstances: a) if continuing the representation will result in a violation of law or a violation of the rules; b) if the client fires her; or c) if she becomes incapacitated.

Q: *And "may* **withdraw?***"*

A: Your lawyer may **withdraw** at any time for no reason, so long as the withdrawal does not cause the client harm. Your lawyer may also **withdraw** if you fail to fulfill an obligation of the representation—don't cooperate in providing information, fail to meet with the lawyer and—this one's important—fail to pay your lawyer.

Q: *Are there more?*

A: A few. Your lawyer is free to **withdraw** if the two of you have irreconcilable differences.

Q: *An example?*

A: You don't want to grant an extension of time to the other side. The lawyer, knowing someday she'll need one, insists as a matter of courtesy.

Q: *Right. You lawyers scratching each other's backs. You said a few?*

A: Yes. If you pursue a course of conduct that your lawyer finds repugnant, she may **withdraw.**

Q: *I thought the client got to decide the ends of the representation? Sounds like the lawyer has a veto.*

A: Not really. This rule only comes into play when the client engages in outrageous conduct such as repeatedly undermining the lawyer's authority or embarrassing the lawyer after the lawyer gave her word on an important matter. We also never talked about one more form of client lying.

Q: *What's that?*

A: If a client lies about something important in a court proceeding or deposition, the lawyer has a duty of candor to the tribunal that requires the lawyer to correct the record.

Q: *So the lawyer's a tattletale?*

A: You could say that. Though you hope it never comes to that. When a lawyer knows her client is lying, the first thing the lawyer must do is talk to the client and ask her to make a correction. Figure out the least dangerous way to do it. It is only if the client refuses to make the correction herself that the lawyer has this absolute obligation to correct the record.

Q: *Even if I fire the lawyer?*

A: Even if you fire the lawyer. And until the correction is made, your lawyer is not allowed to settle your case, just in case you thought that might solve the problem. The other side is entitled to know that fact before it settles, even if there is a settlement offer on the table.

Q: *You know what amuses me? With all these rules about aiding and abetting, lawyers will be scared to give clients advice at all.*

A: We understand what you are saying. But the rules make it clear that the client is entitled to candid advice about the proposed course of conduct. You can ask your lawyer if it is legal to take a certain tax deduction. You can also ask your lawyer the chances of getting caught. Those questions should elicit accurate answers and an admonition to follow the law. What the lawyer cannot do is prepare the tax return that includes an illegal deduction. One is advice; the other aiding and abetting.

YOUR LAWYER CANNOT VIOLATE COURT RULES OR PROCEDURES

Q: *I came out of the hospital a mess. They totally botched my surgery, gave me a terrible infection, which kept me out of work for months. Then they refused to speak to me about any of it. I'm ready to sue them all but I've been to three different lawyers who all refuse to take my case. What gives?*

A: You have every right to seek legal relief, but when lawyers use the courts, they are required to obey **court rules and procedures**. When lawyers represent you in court, they must avoid frivolous lawsuits, those without factual or legal validity. While your anger is understandable, these lawyers may have consulted medical experts who were not prepared to testify that what happened to you constitutes medical malpractice.

Q: *But people lose lawsuits all the time. All I want is a bite at the apple.*

A: True, and perhaps another lawyer will see your case differently. But before filing the lawsuit, the lawyer must conduct research and determine whether there is a good faith basis to proceed.

Q: *I own a small business and I got sued by a disgruntled former employee who claimed that I fired her without good reason. Then during* *what you lawyers call "discovery," the ex-employee demanded to see her confidential employee file. The nerve!*

A: The purpose of discovery is exactly that: to discover the relevant facts in the case. We suspect that your former employee's personnel file might be relevant to her firing. Discovery is also regulated by **court rules** that require lawyers and clients to turn over relevant requested documents even when (or especially when) they would rather not. If you or your lawyer fail to do so, either or both of you could be subject to monetary fines, and worse, dismissal of your defense.

"If you want justice, it's two hundred dollars an hour. Obstruction of justice runs a bit more."

PART FOUR

OTHER PEOPLE'S LAWYERS

CHAPTER 10:
DEALING WITH OTHER
PEOPLE'S LAWYERS

OPPOSING PARTIES: WHY HIRING A LAWYER GIVES YOU SPECIAL PROTECTION FROM THE OTHER SIDE'S LAWYER

Q: *I'm sick and tired of that insurance person bugging me about settling the accident case that hurt my back last month. What can I do?*

A: I know it sounds like pure self-promotion, but one great reason to hire a lawyer is so you don't have to deal with the lawyer on the other side yourself. There is an ethics rule that says a lawyer may not contact the client on the other side without the permission of that client's lawyer.

Q: *So if you represent my company, the lawyer on the other side can't contact any of my employees?*

A: Not quite. It's a little complicated, but once we represent your company, the adverse lawyer cannot talk to some of your employees. Those, like you, who deal with us on the questions relating to the matter, or any employees whose conduct is involved in the matter. Think about your company sued in a truck accident. The lawyer can't contact the truck driver, but could contact your relief driver riding in the back.

Q: *What if my lawyer's the problem? And I want to talk to the lawyer on the other side?*

A: She shouldn't talk to you without your lawyer's permission.

Q: *But I don't want my lawyer to know.*

A: Then you have to fire your lawyer.

Q: *Will the other lawyer then talk to me?*

A: Only when the other side's lawyer confirms that your lawyer knows she's fired.

Q: *How paternalistic!*

A: We would say protective. Remember, the other side's lawyer has her client's best interest at heart, not yours. We don't want vulnerable clients talking to the lawyer on the other side before the clients hear from their lawyer why that is not advisable.

Q: *What if we think the lawyer on the other side isn't passing on our settlement offers?*

A: If you want to be sure your settlement offers are getting through, there is a way.

Q: *What's that?*

A: You, the client, can talk to the other client directly. That's always permissible.

QUESTIONS TO ASK OTHER PEOPLE'S LAWYERS
1. Are you my lawyer?
2. Whose lawyer are you?
3. I have my own lawyer, why aren't you talking to him or her?
4. What do you advise I do?

TALKING TO THE OTHER SIDE'S LAWYER

Q: *What if I decide against hiring my own lawyer in my divorce because it's too expensive?*

A: While the lawyer on the other side cannot talk to you outside the presence of your lawyer without your lawyer's permission, you certainly might end up dealing with the other side's lawyer, either because your lawyer and you decide a meeting between you with that lawyer is a good idea (admittedly a rare event) or because clients and lawyers often meet together for negotiations or depositions or outside the courtroom. Keeping in mind that that lawyer's duties are to her client just as your lawyer's duties are to you, nonetheless, there are two obligations that lawyer owes to you that are worth highlighting here.

First, that lawyer, if she makes statements of fact to you, must be truthful. All lawyers must be truthful to all third parties. That includes the party on the other side.

Second, if that lawyer promises to your lawyer or you to take some action—think about agreeing to hold a deposit, file a deed, record a lease—the other side's lawyer owes *you* a duty to complete the task in a proper way, and failure of the lawyer to do so could result in a claim against that lawyer—even though she was representing the other side.

Q: *What if I am involved in a matter and not represented? I'm a witness ... something like that.*

A: Lawyers also have special obligations to people who are unrepresented. The most important is that a lawyer has to make it clear who she represents and what her interest in the matter is. If the lawyer is from the IRS, you are entitled to know that. And the fact that she is there to get more money from you. Next, the lawyer has to make sure that she does not give you legal advice. Doing so might turn you into a client—and a non-paying one at that.

Q: *Too bad. As I told you, I love free advice.*

A: It may be worth exactly what you're paying for it, so don't love it too much. And there is one exception.

Q: *You lawyers and your exceptions!*

A: The exception is that, if you are unrepresented, the lawyer may give you advice, and in some cases, is really required to give you advice, but that advice has to be limited: to get your own lawyer.

Q: *No more taking advantage of unrepresented people. Bet some lawyers hate that.*

A: You might think so. But the truth is, it's very difficult for lawyers to deal with people who are unrepresented. Most lawyers most of the time would rather deal with individuals through their lawyers.

Q: *Increase the revenues of the club, right?*

A: Not really. It's just very hard to pull out the stops representing your own client if you have to worry about how well the **unrepresented person** understands the situation. It's also hard to follow the rule of not giving advice.

EMPLOYEES AND CORPORATE COUNSEL

Q: *You said there might be times when a lawyer might have to tell an* **unrepresented person** *to get a lawyer.*

A: Right. This refers to a relatively common situation. An employer company is involved in a matter. The company is represented. The lawyer deals with many company employees—could be the CEO, the plant superintendent or a truck driver for the company. Maybe that person is being deposed. And the lawyer for the company is preparing the person for this important event. That lawyer should clarify whether she represents the employee or only the company. Assuming the lawyer does not represent the employee, she should tell the employee not to rely on her and to get her own lawyer.

Q: *What happens if the company lawyer doesn't do this?*

A: If the employee reasonably relied on the lawyer for legal advice, a court could later find that a real client-lawyer relationship, complete with **the 4 Cs**, was created. That means that the employee may be able to seek legal relief if something goes wrong.

PROSECUTORS AND VICTIMS

Q: *My son got mugged in the park last month. Now my wife, son, and I all have been dealing with this young **prosecutor**. She seems sympathetic but I get the sense this mugger is going to get off way too light. If it were up to me, I'd lock him up and throw away the key.*

A: You have learned an important—albeit somewhat painful—lesson. The prosecutors do not represent the victims. While they need victim cooperation and they are often sympathetic, do not confuse that response with the notion that they are your lawyer or take direction from you. They do not. If you want to reinforce the strength of your message, maybe you need to hire your own lawyer to lean on the **prosecutor** or otherwise protect your interests.

INSURANCE LAWYERS

Q: *I had a fender bender last week. My neck's stiff but my doctor says I'll be OK. I heard from this person for the other driver's insurance company. She says the insurance company will promptly process my claim. Not to worry and, whatever I do, don't waste money hiring a lawyer. Sounds like good advice.*

A: It might be, but then again … if that person was a lawyer, she does not represent you. And she broke the first rule of dealing with an **unrepresented person** by giving you advice, maybe even misrepresenting her interest. A non-lawyer claims adjuster can talk to you directly, but if you hire your own lawyer, he cannot. Your lawyer takes the calls and protects your interests. You don't have to have a lawyer but, whatever you do, remember this person is representing a company that wants to pay you as little as possible.

PART FIVE

GAINING EVEN WHEN YOU LOSE

CHAPTER 11:
WHAT IS A SUCCESSFUL CLIENT-LAWYER RELATIONSHIP?

This Almanac has described your lawyer's obligations to you. Before we close, however, a few notes regarding how to judge whether you have received what you are entitled to from your lawyer. Of course you now know to expect **the 4 Cs**: good **communication**, **competence**, **confidentiality**, and **conflict of interest** resolution, and the other obligations we have described. Yet we recognize that in the end, having come to a lawyer to accomplish some goal — to press or defend a claim, buy a home, start a business, get a divorce, whatever — you will not only judge the lawyer's performance by the return of phone calls, but also by the results. In that regard we hasten to remind you of two things.

First, your lawyer should be your one true advocate. If it is the sale of a business, your lawyer should strive to get what matters to you, whether it be top dollar, no future liability, or a clean break. If it is suing for damages from a car accident, your lawyer should try to maximize your recovery, get all your medical costs reimbursed, collect damages for your pain and suffering. If it is a divorce, your lawyer should do his best to get what you want for your future: custody of the children, child support, alimony. Undoubtedly, your lawyer will advocate for all these. You will even have many opportunities to watch your lawyer advocate. He will undoubtedly sound enthusiastic. You will even be convinced by your lawyer's rhetoric. After all, who is more deserving than you?

Second, while your lawyer will also try to achieve the absolute best for you, your lawyer owes you two important obligations. Your lawyer must be candid with you about the strengths and weaknesses of your position. Your lawyer also must recommend a compromise or set-tlement of your matter if the lawyer believes that is in your best inter-ests. When your lawyer does so, do not confuse that advice with any lack of commitment to your cause on your lawyer's part. Your lawyer is in a dual role, advocating for the best and, at the same time, trying to remain realistic about your prospects. If the lawyer were not realistic, the lawyer would violate the duty to **communicate**. So if your lawyer offers advice you don't like, please don't shoot the messenger. Or think that your lawyer is abandoning you when all your lawyer is doing is fulfilling his ethical duty to you.

EVALUATING YOUR LAWYER
1. Did my lawyer charge me the fee I expected? (Chapter 3)
2. Did my lawyer **communicate** well with me? (Chapter 4)
3. Did my lawyer handle my case **competently?** (Chapter 5)
4. Did my lawyer keep my confidences? (Chapter 6)
5. Did my lawyer disclose and resolve **conflicts of interest?** (Chapter 7)
6. If I expressed disappointment with something in my case, did my lawyer explain it to my satisfaction? (Chapter 8)
7. Did my lawyer refuse to assist me if I suggested something illegal? (Chapter 9)
8. Was the outcome of my case, even if not exactly what I expected, satisfactory? (Chapter 11)

DEALING WITH UNCERTAINTY: COST, LEGAL PROCESS, AND OUTCOME

Please remember one thing. You should not let your lawyer's eloquent advocacy for your cause create unrealistic expectations and, therefore, disappointment with what in fact is achieved. While your lawyer may seek $100,000 on your behalf and even argue persuasively that you are entitled to that amount, this does not mean you did not achieve an excellent result when the jury awarded you $50,000.

WHAT DOES IT MEAN TO "WIN"? VICTORY IS NOT ALWAYS A MAXIMUM RECOVERY

A corollary to the foregoing is how you, the client, define victory. It could be that you define it as winning the maximum amount after a jury trial, an appeal or two and the denial by the United States Supreme Court of review of your splendid result. It could be that you define it as your ex-spouse never seeing your children again and throwing your ex into debtor's prison for failing to pay $20,000/month in alimony.

It could be getting 50% more than you expected for the sale of your business.

There is nothing wrong with that. But one thing your lawyer should provide is some broader perspective on what constitutes "victory." It is true that sometimes maximizing recovery is the best you can do. It is true that complete vindication can taste so sweet. But it is also true that such total victory can provide a great short-term benefit but a long-term result of dubious merit. A known settlement can avoid a lot of uncertainty, aggravation and expense as one faces the inability to predict what juries and appellate judges may do. Denying visitation to your ex-spouse can feel like vindication, but can leave the children resentful and deprived. Selling for the top dollar can put money in the bank quickly, but might leave you exposed to contingent liabilities that create anxiety and erode the benefits of an exalted sale price. Not disclosing a property flaw might bring you immediate gain, which might come at the expense of a later **fraud** allegation. It is your lawyer's duty to point these considerations out to you, and it is you, because you are the ultimate decision-maker, who should consider that advice and then be prepared to live with the consequences, whatever they may be. While we would never suggest the slightest compromise with the fundamental principle that the client gets to decide the objectives of the representation, one benefit a client receives by retaining a lawyer is the objectivity a third person can provide that few, if any, of us possess once we are involved in a matter where we require the help of a lawyer.

VICTORY IS NOT THE END

Q: *I've got everything I want now. The jury came in with a verdict of $75,000 and $150,000 in punitive damages. I'm so glad I didn't listen to my lawyer and settle for $100,000.*

A: You still may want to settle.

Q: *After such a victory? The jury was only out for two hours!*

A: Even with a satisfying jury verdict, you may want to compromise. As they say there are many slips twixt the cup and lip. With that large a verdict the other side will surely file what are called post trial motions, requests that the judge set the verdict aside. Then there are appeals. Depending on the state you're in, there could be two levels of appeal. Even if you won those, you are still not guaranteed your just desserts. All you'll have is a judgment. Turning that into cash may require further proceedings and the defendant may not have assets that are easy to grab. Moreover, the defendant could go into bankruptcy, a bleak avenue that could result in your receiving just pennies on the dollar and then only after months of waiting. So we're not saying don't try to secure the entire sum the jury awarded. Just keep in mind that sometimes the better victory might be a certain result. The point: You have to live with the outcome, and you get to decide what to do. And you are entitled to your lawyer's advice about all of these considerations before you choose.

ALTERNATIVE DISPUTE RESOLUTION: A PRACTICAL SOLUTION?

Q: *I've got this great claim for damages and now my swashbuckling trial lawyer seems to have morphed into a whimpering negotiator. He wants us to go to **mediation**. Doesn't sound like a process designed to vindicate my claim.*

A: There is no doubt that **mediation** is to trial as skim milk is to 100-proof tequila. But everything is a tradeoff. A mediated settlement might get you a perfectly satisfactory and more complete or certain result. And it may give you the opportunity to articulate your real interests in a much less threatening environment. For many clients, this may be better than the chance to obtain more money at a public trial. That alternative, while undoubtedly inducing an adrenaline rush and providing the only way the amount you receive is not compromised, also involves aggravation, delay, uncertainty, and more control by lawyers, no matter how strong your case or how outsized your damage claim. As you think about how disappointed you will be if you mediate to a result that achieves only half a loaf, also contemplate how you will feel if a defense verdict leaves you walking out of the courthouse empty-handed. It is, of course, your choice but when your lawyer asks you to think hard about **mediation** and then asks you to consider seriously a mediated result, don't reject the advice out of hand or confuse your lawyer's sage advice with any lack of lawyer ardor for your cause.

APPENDIX 1:
LAWYER REFERRAL SERVICES TO HELP
YOU FIND A LAWYER

NAME	FEATURES	HOW LAWYERS ARE LISTED	WEBSITE
ABA: Find Legal Help	■ ABA website to connect people to lawyer referral sites and legal information ■ Ability to connect to state/city bar association lawyer referral services and for-profit directories ■ Provides links for free legal help and self help	■ This website is run by the American Bar Association ■ The non-profit referral sites specify whether or not they meet with the ABA standards for lawyer referral ■ Membership in these referral services is open to all licensed lawyers who belong to the local bar association) ■ Some local bar associations have subject matter panels that establish minimum standards for eligibility	www.findlegalhelp.org

NAME	FEATURES	HOW LAWYERS ARE LISTED	WEBSITE
American Lawyer Referral	■ Can search by state, county and practice area ■ Will provides names, contact information and practice area	■ Lawyers either pay to be listed, or may provide a reciprocal link to American Lawyer Referral on the lawyer's website for free listings.	www.americanlawyerreferral.com
Best Lawyers	■ Can search by country, state, city, specialty, subspecialty, firm, and/or name. ■ Results for browsing cities and practice areas will return the names of lawyers who have paid to be listed, however, if you search for particular lawyers by name, any lawyer included in the site will show up.	■ The selection process is based on peer review. Lawyers are asked, "If you couldn't handle a case yourself, who would you refer it to?" and then are asked to grade the response-lawyer with either an A, B, or C (can use + & -). ■ Best Lawyers then checks the finalists at the state ethics board and gets the lawyer's information. ■ This site ranks less than 5% of the lawyers in each state.	www.BestLawyers.com Book also available: The Best Lawyers in America 2008 (new editions published yearly)
FindLaw	■ Can search by city, state, legal issue, name, or a combination ■ Also has option of submitting your legal issue and having a lawyer contact you	■ This site is run by the same company that runs Westlaw, a for-profit legal research database ■ Lawyers pay to be listed, and the more attractive spots are gained by payment of more money—not a better ranking	www.findlaw.com

NAME	FEATURES	HOW LAWYERS ARE LISTED	WEBSITE
Lawyers.com	■ Can search by city/state/country, practice area, name ■ Includes legal research information ■ Search results include detailed biography, maps to offices, firm information ■ Includes link to "Ask a Lawyer" questions	■ This website is run by the same company that runs Lexis Nexis, a for-profit legal research database ■ Lawyers pay to be listed, and the more attractive spots are gained by extra payment—not a better ranking	www.lawyers.com
Martindale-Hubbell	■ Can browse lawyers by location, practice area, name ■ Includes ratings & categories ■ Has a Top 10 List (by Peer Review Rating, Activity, Visibility)	■ Banner results that call attention to specific law firms, photos or logos are a result of payment—not rankings ■ Lawyers pay for listings and inclusion in Martindale-Hubbell	www.martindale.com Book also available: Martindale-Hubbell Law Directory

NAME	FEATURES	HOW LAWYERS ARE LISTED	WEBSITE
Super Lawyers	■ Can browse by practice area, state, keyword, name or city ■ Provides links to the Attorney General and State Bars ■ Information provided for search results: years of practice, law school, practice areas ■ Also available in book format	■ There is an initial statewide survey for nominations of top lawyers, then Super Lawyers researches nominees based on a lengthy criteria list. Then Peer Review occurs by practice area. Lastly, Super Lawyers checks for state licenses, disciplinary history and other possible outstanding issues. ■ Lawyers can pay for profile extras (pictures, premium placement, issues, etc.). ■ This group ranks only the Top 5% of lawyers in each state.	www.superlawyers. com Each participating state also has a magazine published each year listing that state's Super Lawyers (AZ, AK, CT, CO, FL, GA, IL, IN, KS, LA, MD, MA, MI, MS, MO, NJ, NY, NC, Northern CA, OH, OK, OR, PA, Southern CA, TN, TX, VA and WI.

APPENDIX 2:
SELECTED SECTIONS OF THE
RESTATEMENT (THIRD) OF THE LAW
GOVERNING LAWYERS (2000)*

Note: The Restatement sections set forth here state general propositions of law that have been adopted in the majority of states. The law where you live might be different.

§ 14. FORMATION OF A CLIENT-LAWYER RELATIONSHIP

A relationship of client and lawyer arises when:

(1) a person manifests to a lawyer the person's intent that the lawyer provide legal services for the person; and either

    (a) the lawyer manifests to the person consent to do so; or

    (b) the lawyer fails to manifest lack of consent to do so, and the lawyer knows or reasonably should know that the person reasonably relies on the lawyer to provide the services; or

(2) a tribunal with power to do so appoints the lawyer to provide the services.

§ 16. A LAWYER'S DUTIES TO A CLIENT—IN GENERAL

To the extent consistent with the lawyer's other legal duties and subject to the other provisions of this Restatement, a lawyer must, in matters within the scope of the representation:

(1) proceed in a manner reasonably calculated to advance a client's lawful objectives, as defined by the client after consultation;

(2) act with reasonable competence and diligence;

(3) comply with obligations concerning the client's confidences and property, avoid impermissible conflicting interests, deal honestly with the client, and not employ advantages arising from the client-lawyer relationship in a manner adverse to the client; and

(4) fulfill valid contractual obligations to the client.

§ 17. A CLIENT'S DUTIES TO A LAWYER

Subject to the other provisions of this Restatement, in matters covered by the representation a client must:

(1) compensate a lawyer for services and expenses as stated in Chapter 3;

(2) indemnify the lawyer for liability to which the client has exposed the lawyer without the lawyer's fault; and

(3) fulfill any valid contractual obligations to the lawyer.

§ 18. CLIENT-LAWYER CONTRACTS

(1) A contract between a lawyer and client concerning the client-lawyer relationship, including a contract modifying an existing contract, may be enforced by either party if the contract meets other applicable requirements, except that:

    (a) if the contract or modification is made beyond a reasonable time after the lawyer has begun to represent the client in the matter (see § 38(1)), the client may avoid it unless the lawyer shows that the contract and the circumstances of its formation were fair and reasonable to the client; and

    (b) if the contract is made after the lawyer has finished providing services, the client may avoid it if the client was not informed of facts needed to evaluate the appropriateness of the lawyer's compensation or other benefits conferred on the lawyer by the contract.

(2) A tribunal should construe a contract between client and lawyer as a reasonable person in the circumstances of the client would have construed it.

§ 19. AGREEMENTS LIMITING CLIENT OR LAWYER DUTIES

(1) Subject to other requirements stated in this Restatement, a client and lawyer may agree to limit a duty that a lawyer would otherwise owe to the client if:

    (a) the client is adequately informed and consents; and

(b) the terms of the limitation are reasonable in the circumstances.

(2) A lawyer may agree to waive a client's duty to pay or other duty owed to the lawyer.

§ 20. A LAWYER'S DUTY TO INFORM AND CONSULT WITH A CLIENT

(1) A lawyer must keep a client reasonably informed about the matter and must consult with a client to a reasonable extent concerning decisions to be made by the lawyer under §§ 21-23.

(2) A lawyer must promptly comply with a client's reasonable requests for information.

(3) A lawyer must notify a client of decisions to be made by the client under §§ 21-23 and must explain a matter to the extent reasonably necessary to permit the client to make informed decisions regarding the representation.

§ 21. ALLOCATING THE AUTHORITY TO DECIDE BETWEEN A CLIENT AND A LAWYER

As between client and lawyer:

(1) A client and lawyer may agree which of them will make specified decisions, subject to the requirements stated in §§ 18, 19, 22, 23, and other provisions of this Restatement. The agreement may be superseded by another valid agreement.

(2) A client may instruct a lawyer during the representation, subject to the requirements stated in §§ 22, 23, and other provisions of this Restatement.

(3) Subject to Subsections (1) and (2) a lawyer may take any lawful measure within the scope of representation that is reasonably calculated to advance a client's objectives as defined by the client, consulting with the client as required by § 20.

(4) A client may ratify an act of a lawyer that was not previously authorized.

§ 22. AUTHORITY RESERVED TO A CLIENT

(1) As between client and lawyer, subject to Subsection (2) and § 23, the following and comparable decisions are reserved to the client except when the client has validly authorized the lawyer to make the particular decision: whether and on what terms to settle a claim; how a criminal defendant should plead; whether a criminal defendant should waive jury trial; whether a criminal defendant should testify; and whether to appeal in a civil proceeding or criminal prosecution.

(2) A client may not validly authorize a lawyer to make the decisions described in Subsection (1) when other law (such as criminal-procedure rules governing pleas, jury-trial waiver, and defendant testimony) requires the client's personal participation or approval.

(3) Regardless of any contrary contract with a lawyer, a client may revoke a lawyer's authority to make the decisions described in Subsection (1).

§ 23. AUTHORITY RESERVED TO A LAWYER

As between client and lawyer, a lawyer retains authority that may not be overridden by a contract with or an instruction from the client:

(1) to refuse to perform, counsel, or assist future or ongoing acts in the representation that the lawyer reasonably believes to be unlawful;

(2) to make decisions or take actions in the representation that the lawyer reasonably believes to be required by law or an order of a tribunal.

§ 38. CLIENT-LAWYER FEE CONTRACTS

(1) Before or within a reasonable time after beginning to represent a client in a matter, a lawyer must communicate to the client, in writing when applicable rules so provide, the basis or rate of the fee, unless the communication is unnecessary for the client because the lawyer has previously represented that client on the same basis or at the same rate.

(2) The validity and construction of a contract between a client and a lawyer concerning the lawyer's fees are governed by § 18.

(3) Unless a contract construed in the circumstances indicates otherwise:

(a) a lawyer may not charge separately for the lawyer's general office and overhead expenses;

(b) payments that the law requires an opposing party or that party's lawyer to pay as attorney-fee awards or sanctions are credited to the client, not the client's lawyer, absent a contrary statute or court order; and

(c) when a lawyer requests and receives a fee payment that is not for services already rendered, that payment is to be credited against whatever fee the lawyer is entitled to collect.

§ 39. A LAWYER'S FEE IN THE ABSENCE OF A CONTRACT

If a client and lawyer have not made a valid contract providing for another measure of compensation, a client owes a lawyer who has performed legal services for the client the fair value of the lawyer's services.

§ 40. FEES ON TERMINATION

If a client-lawyer relationship ends before the lawyer has completed the services due for a matter and the lawyer's fee has not been forfeited under § 37:

(1) a lawyer who has been discharged or withdraws may recover the lesser of the fair value of the lawyer's services as determined under § 39 and the ratable proportion of the compensation provided by any otherwise enforceable contract between lawyer and client for the services performed; except that

(2) the tribunal may allow such a lawyer to recover the ratable proportion of the compensation provided by such a contract if:

(a) the discharge or withdrawal is not attributable to misconduct of the lawyer;

(b) the lawyer has performed severable services; and

(c) allowing contractual compensation would not burden the client's choice of counsel or the client's ability to replace counsel.

§ 46. DOCUMENTS RELATING TO A REPRESENTATION

(1) A lawyer must take reasonable steps to safeguard documents in the lawyer's possession relating to the representation of a client or former client.

(2) On request, a lawyer must allow a client or former client to inspect and copy any document possessed by the lawyer relating to the representation, unless substantial grounds exist to refuse.

(3) Unless a client or former client consents to nondelivery or substantial grounds exist for refusing to make delivery, a lawyer must deliver to the client or former client, at an appropriate time and in any event promptly after the representation ends, such originals and copies of other documents possessed by the lawyer relating to the representation as the client or former client reasonably needs.

(4) Notwithstanding Subsections (2) and (3), a lawyer may decline to deliver to a client or former client an original or copy of any document under circumstances permitted by § 43(1).

§ 116. INTERVIEWING AND PREPARING A PROSPECTIVE WITNESS

(1) A lawyer may interview a witness for the purpose of preparing the witness to testify.

(2) A lawyer may not unlawfully obstruct another party's access to a witness.

(3) A lawyer may not unlawfully induce or assist a prospective witness to evade or ignore process obliging the witness to appear to testify.

(4) A lawyer may not request a person to refrain from voluntarily giving relevant testimony or information to another party, unless:

    (a) the person is the lawyer's client in the matter; or

    (b) (i) the person is not the lawyer's client but is a relative or employee or other agent of the lawyer or the lawyer's client, and

        (ii) the lawyer reasonably believes compliance will not materially and adversely affect the person's interests.

§ 117. COMPENSATING A WITNESS

A lawyer may not offer or pay to a witness any consideration:

(1) in excess of the reasonable expenses of the witness incurred and the reasonable value of the witness's time spent in providing evidence, except that an expert witness may be offered and paid a noncontingent fee;

(2) contingent on the content of the witness's testimony or the outcome of the litigation; or

(3) otherwise prohibited by law.

§ 118. FALSIFYING OR DESTROYING EVIDENCE

(1) A lawyer may not falsify documentary or other evidence.

(2) A lawyer may not destroy or obstruct another party's access to documentary or other evidence when doing so would violate a court order or other legal requirements, or counsel or assist a client to do so.

§ 119. PHYSICAL EVIDENCE OF A CLIENT CRIME

With respect to physical evidence of a client crime, a lawyer:

(1) may, when reasonably necessary for purposes of the representation, take possession of the evidence and retain it for the time reasonably necessary to examine it and subject it to tests that do not alter or destroy material characteristics of the evidence; but

(2) following possession under Subsection (1), the lawyer must notify prosecuting authorities of the lawyer's possession of the evidence or turn the evidence over to them.

APPENDIX 3:
SELECTED PROVISIONS OF REPRESENTATIVE STATE RULES OF PROFESSIONAL CONDUCT

Note: Each state has its own rules of professional conduct. The rules below are representative of most state rules, but the exact rule in any state may differ significantly from the provision in this appendix. To view the exact rules of professional conduct for lawyers in your state, go to the website listed in Appendix 4.

ARKANSAS RULE OF PROFESSIONAL CONDUCT RULE 1.1:

Competence

A lawyer shall provide competent representation to a client. Competent representation requires the legal knowledge, skill, thoroughness and preparation reasonably necessary for the representation.

IOWA RULE OF PROFESSIONAL CONDUCT 1.2:

Scope Of Representation And Allocation Of Authority Between Client And Lawyer

(a) Subject to paragraphs (c) and (d), a lawyer shall abide by a client's decisions concerning the objectives of representation and, as required by rule 1.4, shall consult with the client as to the means by which they are to be pursued. A lawyer may take such action on behalf of the client as is impliedly authorized to carry out the representation. A lawyer shall abide by a client's decision whether to settle a matter.

In a criminal case, the lawyer shall abide by the client's decision, after consultation with the lawyer, as to a plea to be entered, whether to waive jury trial, and whether the client will testify.

(b) A lawyer's representation of a client, including representation by appointment, does not constitute an endorsement of the client's political, economic, social, or moral views or activities.

(c) A lawyer may limit the scope of the representation if the limitation is reasonable under the circumstances and the client gives informed consent.

(d) A lawyer shall not counsel a client to engage, or assist a client, in conduct that the lawyer knows is criminal or fraudulent, but a lawyer may discuss the legal consequences of any proposed course of conduct with a client and may counsel or assist a client to make a good faith effort to determine the validity, scope, meaning, or application of the law.

COLORADO RULE OF PROFESSIONAL CONDUCT 1.3:

Diligence

A lawyer shall act with reasonable diligence and promptness in representing a client.

NEBRASKA RULE OF PROFESSIONAL CONDUCT 1.4:

Communications

(a) A lawyer shall:

(1) promptly inform the client of any decision or circumstance with respect to which the client's informed consent, as defined in Rule 1.0(e), is required by these Rules;

(2) reasonably consult with the client about the means by which the client's objectives are to be accomplished;

(3) keep the client reasonably informed about the status of the matter;

(4) promptly comply with reasonable requests for information; and

(5) consult with the client about any relevant limitation on the lawyer's conduct when the lawyer knows that the client expects assistance not permitted by the Rules of Professional Conduct or other law.

(b) A lawyer shall explain a matter to the extent reasonably necessary to permit the client to make informed decisions regarding the representation.

MISSOURI RULE OF PROFESSIONAL CONDUCT 1.5:

Fees

(a) A lawyer shall not make an agreement for, charge, or collect an unreasonable fee or an unreasonable amount for expenses. The factors to be considered in determining the reasonableness of a fee include the following:

(1) the time and labor required, the novelty and difficulty of the questions involved, and the skill requisite to perform the legal service properly;

(2) the likelihood, if apparent to the client, that the acceptance of the particular employment will preclude other employment by the lawyer;

(3) the fee customarily charged in the locality for similar legal services;

(4) the amount involved and the results obtained;

(5) the time limitations imposed by the client or by the circumstances;

(6) the nature and length of the professional relationship with the client;

(7) the experience, reputation, and ability of the lawyer or lawyers performing the services; and

(8) whether the fee is fixed or contingent.

(b) The scope of the representation and the basis or rate of the fee and expenses for which the client will be responsible shall be communicated to the client, preferably in writing, before or within a reasonable time after commencing the representation, except when the lawyer will charge a regularly represented client on the same basis or rate. Any changes in the basis or rate of the fee or expenses shall also be communicated to the client.

(c) A fee may be contingent on the outcome of the matter for which the service is rendered, except in a matter in which a contingent fee is prohibited by Rule []1.5(d) or other law. A contingent fee agreement shall be in a writing signed by the client and shall state the method by which the fee is to be determined, including the percentage or percentages that shall accrue to the lawyer in the event of settlement, trial or appeal; litigation and other expenses to be deducted from the recovery; and whether such expenses are to be deducted before or after the contingent fee is calculated. The agreement must clearly notify the client of any expenses for which the client will be liable whether or not the client is the prevailing party. Upon conclusion of a contingent fee matter, the lawyer shall provide the client with a written statement stating the outcome of the matter and, if there is a recovery, showing the remittance to the client and the method of its determination.

(d) A lawyer shall not enter into an arrangement for, charge, or collect:

(1) any fee in a domestic relations matter the payment or amount of which is contingent upon the securing of a divorce or dissolution of the marriage or upon the amount of maintenance, alimony or support or property settlement in lieu thereof; or

(2) a contingent fee for representing a defendant in a criminal case.

(e) A division of a fee between lawyers who are not in the same firm may be made only if:

(1) the division is in proportion to the services performed by each lawyer or each lawyer assumes joint responsibility for the representation;

(2) the client agrees to the association and the agreement is confirmed in writing; and

(3) the total fee is reasonable.

DELAWARE RULE OF PROFESSIONAL CONDUCT 1.6:

Confidentiality of Information

(a) A lawyer shall not reveal information relating to the representation of a client unless the client gives informed consent, the disclosures is impliedly authorized in order to carry out the representation, or the disclosure is permitted by paragraph (b).

(b) A lawyer may reveal information relating to the representation of a client to the extent the lawyer reasonably believes necessary:

(1) to prevent reasonably certain death or substantial bodily harm;

(2) to prevent the client from committing a crime or fraud that is reasonably certain to result in substantial injury to the financial interests or property of another and in furtherance of which the client has used or is using the lawyer's services;

(3) to prevent, mitigate, or rectify substantial injury to the financial interests or property of another that is reasonably certain to result or has resulted from the client's commission of a crime or fraud in furtherance of which the client has used the lawyer's services;

(4) to secure legal advice about the lawyer's compliance with these Rules;

(5) to establish a claim or defense on behalf of the lawyer in a controversy between the lawyer and the client, to establish a defense to a criminal charge or civil claim against the lawyer based upon conduct in which the client was involved, or to respond to allegations in any proceeding concerning the lawyer's representation of the client; or

(6) to comply with other law or a court order.

INDIANA RULE OF PROFESSIONAL CONDUCT 1.7:

Conflict of Interest: Current Clients

(a) Except as provided in paragraph (b), a lawyer shall not represent a client if the representation involves a concurrent conflict of interest. A concurrent conflict of interest exists if:

(1) the representation of one client will be directly adverse to another client; or

(2) there is a significant risk that the representation of one or more clients will be materially limited by the lawyer's responsibilities to another client, a former client or a third person or by a personal interest of the lawyer.

(b) Notwithstanding the existence of a concurrent conflict of interest under paragraph (a), a lawyer may represent a client if:

(1) the lawyer reasonably believes that the lawyer will be able to provide competent and diligent representation to each affected client;

(2) the representation is not prohibited by law;

(3) the representation does not involve the assertion of a claim by one client against another client represented by the lawyer in the same litigation or other proceeding before a tribunal; and

(4) each affected client gives informed consent, confirmed in writing.

NEW HAMPSHIRE RULE OF PROFESSIONAL CONDUCT 1.8:

Conflict of Interest: Current Clients: Specific Rules

(a) A lawyer shall not enter into a business transaction with a client or knowingly acquire an ownership, possessory, security or other pecuniary interest adverse to a client unless:

(1) the transaction and terms on which the lawyer acquires the interest are fair and reasonable to the client and are fully disclosed and transmitted in writing in a manner that can be reasonably understood by the client;

(2) the client is advised in writing of the desirability of seeking and is given a reasonable opportunity to seek the advice of independent legal counsel on the transaction; and

(3) the client gives informed consent, in a writing signed by the client, to the essential terms of the transaction and the lawyer's role in the transaction, including whether the lawyer is representing the client in the transaction.

(b) A lawyer shall not use information relating to representation of a client to the disadvantage of the client unless the client gives informed consent, except as permitted or required by these Rules.

(c) A lawyer shall not solicit any substantial gift from a client, including a testamentary gift, or prepare on behalf of a client an instrument giving the lawyer or a person related to the lawyer any substantial gift unless the lawyer or other recipient of the gift is related to the client. For purposes of this paragraph, related persons include a spouse, child, grandchild, parent, grandparent or other relative or individual with whom the lawyer or the client maintains a close, familial relationship.

(d) Prior to the conclusion of representation of a client, a lawyer shall not make or negotiate an agreement giving the lawyer literary or media rights to a portrayal or account based in substantial part on information relating to the representation.

(e) A lawyer shall not provide financial assistance to a client in connection with pending or contemplated litigation, except that:

(1) a lawyer may advance court costs and expenses of litigation, the repayment of which may be contingent on the outcome of the matter; and

(2) a lawyer representing an indigent client may pay court costs and expenses of litigation on behalf of the client.

(f) A lawyer shall not accept compensation for representing a client from one other than the client unless:

(1) the client gives informed consent;

(2) there is no interference with the lawyer's independence of professional judgment or with the client-lawyer relationship; and

(3) information relating to representation of a client is protected as required by Rule 1.6.

(g) A lawyer who represents two or more clients shall not participate in making an aggregate settlement of the claims of or against the clients, or in a criminal case an aggregated agreement as to guilty or nolo contendere pleas, unless each client gives informed consent, in a writing signed by the client. The lawyer's disclosure shall include the existence and nature of all the claims or pleas involved and of the participation of each person in the settlement.

(h) A lawyer shall not:

(1) make an agreement prospectively limiting the lawyer's liability to a client for malpractice unless the client is independently represented in making the agreement; or

(2) settle a claim or potential claim for such liability with an unrepresented client or former client unless that person is advised in writing of the desirability of seeking and is given a reasonable opportunity to seek the advice of independent legal counsel in connection therewith.

(i) A lawyer shall not acquire a proprietary interest in the cause of action or subject matter of litigation the lawyer is conducting for a client, except that the lawyer may:

(1) acquire a lien authorized by law to secure the lawyer's fee or expenses; and

(2) contract with a client for a reasonable contingent fee in a civil case.

(j) A lawyer shall not have sexual relations with a client unless a consensual sexual relationship existed between them when the client-lawyer relationship commenced.

(k) While lawyers are associated in a firm, a prohibition in the foregoing paragraphs (a) through (i) that applies to any one of them shall apply to all of them.

ARIZONA RULE OF PROFESSIONAL CONDUCT 1.9:

Duties to Former Clients

(a) A lawyer who has formerly represented a client in a matter shall not thereafter represent another person in the same or a substantially related matter in which that person's interests are materially adverse to the interests of the former client unless the former client gives informed consent, confirmed in writing.

(b) A lawyer shall not knowingly represent a person in the same or a substantially related matter in which a firm with which the lawyer formerly was associated had previously represented a client:

(1) whose interests are materially adverse to that person; and

(2) about whom the lawyer had acquired information protected by ERs 1.6 and 1.9(c) that is material to the matter; unless the former client gives informed consent, confirmed in writing.

(c) A lawyer who has formerly represented a client in a matter shall not thereafter:

(1) use information relating to the representation to the disadvantage of the former client except as these Rules would permit or require with respect to a client, or when the information has become generally known; or

(2) reveal information relating to the representation except as these Rules would permit or require with respect to a client.

IDAHO RULES OF PROFESSIONAL CONDUCT 1.10:

Imputation of Conflicts of Interest: General Rule

(a) While lawyers are associated in a firm, none of them shall knowingly represent a client when any one of them practicing alone would be prohibited from doing so by Rules 1.7 or 1.9, unless the prohibition is based on a personal interest of the prohibited lawyer and does not present a significant risk of materially limiting the representation of the client by the remaining lawyers in the firm.

(b) When a lawyer has terminated an association with a firm, the firm is not prohibited from thereafter representing a person with interests materially adverse to those of a client represented by the formerly associated lawyer and not currently represented by the firm, unless:

(1) the matter is the same or substantially related to that in which the formerly associated lawyer represented the client; and

(2) any lawyer remaining in the firm has information protected by Rules 1.6 and 1.9(c) that is material to the matter.

(c) A disqualification prescribed by this rule may be waived by the affected client under the conditions stated in Rule 1.7.

(d) The disqualification of lawyers associated in a firm with former or current government lawyers is governed by Rule 1.11.

UTAH RULE OF PROFESSIONAL CONDUCT 1.15:

Safekeeping of Property

(a) A lawyer shall hold property of clients or third persons that is in a lawyer's possession in connection with a representation separate from the lawyer's own property. Funds shall be kept in a separate account maintained in the state where the lawyer's office is situated or elsewhere with the consent of the client or third person. The account may only be maintained in a financial institution that agrees to report to the Office of Professional Conduct in the event any instrument in properly payable form is presented against an attorney trust account containing insufficient funds, irrespective of whether or not the instrument is honored. Other property shall be identified as such and appropriately safeguarded. Complete records of such account funds and other property shall be kept by the lawyer and shall be preserved for a period of five years after termination of the representation.

(b) A lawyer may deposit the lawyer's own funds in a client trust account for the sole purpose of paying bank service charges on that account, but only in an amount necessary for that purpose.

(c) A lawyer shall deposit into a client trust account legal fees and expenses that have been paid in advance, to be withdrawn by the lawyer only as fees are earned or expenses incurred.

(d) Upon receiving funds or other property in which a client or third person has an interest, a lawyer shall promptly notify the client or third person. Except as stated in this Rule or otherwise permitted by law or by agreement with the client, a lawyer shall promptly deliver to the client or third person any funds or other property that the client or third person is entitled to receive and, upon request by the client or third person, shall promptly render a full accounting regarding such property.

(e) When in the course of representation a lawyer is in possession of property in which two or more persons (one of whom may be the lawyer) claim interests, the property shall be kept separate by the lawyer until the dispute is resolved. The lawyer shall promptly distribute all portions of the property as to which the interests are not in dispute.

PENNSYLVANIA RULE OF PROFESSIONAL CONDUCT 1.16:

Declining or Terminating Representation

(a) Except as stated in paragraph (c), a lawyer shall not represent a client or, where representation has commenced, shall withdraw from the representation of a client if:

(1) the representation will result in violation of the Rules of Professional Conduct or other law;

(2) the lawyer's physical or mental condition materially impairs the lawyer's ability to represent the client; or

(3) the lawyer is discharged.

(b) Except as stated in paragraph (c), a lawyer may withdraw from representing a client if:

(1) withdrawal can be accomplished without material adverse effect on the interests of the client;

(2) the client persists in a course of action involving the lawyer's services that the lawyer reasonably believes is criminal or fraudulent;

(3) the client has used the lawyer's services to perpetrate a crime or fraud;

(4) the client insists upon taking action that the lawyer considers repugnant or with which the lawyer has a fundamental disagreement;

(5) the client fails substantially to fulfill an obligation to the lawyer regarding the lawyer's services and has been given reasonable warning that the lawyer will withdraw unless the obligation is fulfilled;

(6) the representation will result in an unreasonable financial burden on the lawyer or has been rendered unreasonably difficult by the client; or

(7) other good cause for withdrawal exists.

(c) A lawyer must comply with applicable law requiring notice to or permission of a tribunal when terminating a representation. When ordered to do so by a tribunal, a lawyer shall continue representation notwithstanding good cause for terminating the representation.

(d) Upon termination of representation, a lawyer shall take steps to the extent reasonably practicable to protect a client's interests, such as giving reasonable notice to the client, allowing time for employment of other counsel, surrendering papers and property to which the client is entitled and refunding any advance payment of fee or expense that has not been earned or incurred. The lawyer may retain papers relating to the client to the extent permitted by other law.

RHODE ISLAND RULE OF PROFESSIONAL CONDUCT 1.18:

Duties to Prospective Client

(a) A person who discusses with a lawyer the possibility of forming a client-lawyer relationship with respect to a matter is a prospective client.

(b) Even when no client-lawyer relationship ensues, a lawyer who has had discussions with a prospective client shall not use or reveal information learned in the consultation, except as Rule 1.9 would permit with respect to information of a former client.

(c) A lawyer subject to paragraph (b) shall not represent a client with interests materially adverse to those of a prospective client in the same or a substantially related matter if the lawyer received information from the prospective client that could be significantly harmful to that person in the matter, except as provided in paragraph (d). If a lawyer is disqualified from representation under this paragraph, no lawyer in a firm with which that lawyer is associated may knowingly undertake or continue representation in such a matter, except as provided in paragraph (d).

(d) When the lawyer has received disqualifying information as defined in paragraph (c), representation is permissible if:

(1) both the affected client and the prospective client have given informed consent, confirmed in writing, or:

(2) the lawyer who received the information took reasonable measures to avoid exposure to more disqualifying information than was reasonably necessary to determine whether to represent the prospective client; and

(i) the disqualified lawyer is timely screened from any participation in the matter and is apportioned no part of the fee therefrom; and

(ii) written notice is promptly given to the prospective client.

DISTRICT OF COLUMBIA RULE OF PROFESSIONAL CONDUCT 2.1:

Advisor

In representing a client, a lawyer shall exercise independent professional judgment and render candid advice. In rendering advice, a lawyer may refer not only to law but to other considerations such as moral, economic, social, and political factors, that may be relevant to the client's situation.

MINNESOTA RULE OF PROFESSIONAL CONDUCT 3.1:

Meritorious Claims and Contentions

A lawyer shall not bring or defend a proceeding, or assert or controvert an issue therein, unless there is a basis in law and fact for doing so that is not frivolous, which includes a good faith argument for an extension, modification, or reversal of existing law. A lawyer for a defendant in a criminal proceeding, or the respondent in a proceeding that could result in incarceration, may nevertheless so defend the proceeding as to require that every element of the case be established.

CONNECTICUT RULE OF PROFESSIONAL CONDUCT 3.2:

Expediting Litigation

A lawyer shall make reasonable efforts to expedite litigation consistent with the interests of the client.

SOUTH DAKOTA RULE OF PROFESSIONAL CONDUCT 3.3:

Candor Toward the Tribunal

(a) A lawyer shall not knowingly:

(1) make a false statement of fact or law to a tribunal or fail to timely correct a false statement of material fact or law previously made to the tribunal by the lawyer;

(2) fail to disclose to the tribunal legal authority in the controlling jurisdiction known to the lawyer to be directly adverse to the position of the client and not disclosed by opposing counsel; or

(3) offer evidence that the lawyer knows to be false. If a lawyer, the lawyer's client, or a witness called by the lawyer, has offered material evidence and the lawyer comes to know of its falsity, the lawyer shall timely take reasonable remedial measures, including, if necessary, disclosure to the tribunal. A lawyer may refuse to offer evidence, other than the testimony of a defendant in a criminal matter, that the lawyer reasonably believes is false. However, in a criminal matter, the lawyer shall not participate with the client in the presentation of the client's testimony which the lawyer knows to be false.

(b) A lawyer who represents a client in an adjudicative proceeding and who knows that a person intends to engage, is engaging or has engaged in criminal or fraudulent conduct related to the proceeding shall timely take reasonable remedial measures, including, if necessary, disclosure to the tribunal.

(c) The duties stated in paragraphs (a) and (b) continue to the conclusion of the proceeding, and apply even if compliance requires disclosure of information otherwise protected by Rule 1.6.

(d) In an ex parte proceeding, except grand juries and applications for search warrants, a lawyer shall inform the tribunal of all material facts known to the lawyer that will enable the tribunal to make an informed decision, whether or not the facts are adverse.

WISCONSIN RULE OF PROFESSIONAL CONDUCT 3.4:

Fairness to Opposing Party and Counsel

A lawyer shall not:

(a) unlawfully obstruct another party's access to evidence or unlawfully alter, destroy or conceal a document or other material having potential evidentiary value. A lawyer shall not counsel or assist another person to do any such act;

(b) falsify evidence, counsel or assist a witness to testify falsely, or offer an inducement to a witness that is prohibited by law;

(c) knowingly disobey an obligation under the rules of a tribunal, except for an open refusal based on an assertion that no valid obligation exists;

(d) in pretrial procedure, make a frivolous discovery request or fail to make reasonably diligent effort to comply with a legally proper discovery request by an opposing party;

(e) in trial, allude to any matter that the lawyer does not reasonably believe is relevant or that will not be supported by admissible evidence, assert personal knowledge of facts in issue except when testifying as a witness, or state a personal opinion as to the justness of a cause, the credibility of a witness, the culpability of a civil litigant or the guilt or innocence of an accused; or

(f) request a person other than a client to refrain from voluntarily giving relevant information to another party unless:

(1) the person is a relative or an employee or other agent of a client; and

(2) the lawyer reasonably believes that the person's interests will not be adversely affected by refraining from giving such information.

RULE REGULATING THE FLORIDA BAR 4.1:

Truthfulness in Statements to Others

In the course of representing a client a lawyer shall not knowingly:

(a) make a false statement of material fact or law to a third person; or

(b) fail to disclose a material fact to a third person when disclosure is necessary to avoid assisting a criminal or fraudulent act by a client, unless disclosure is prohibited by rule 4-1.6.

WASHINGTON RULE OF PROFESSIONAL CONDUCT 4.2:

Communication with Person Represented by Counsel

In representing a client, a lawyer shall not communicate about the subject of the representation with a person the lawyer knows to be represented by another lawyer in the matter, unless the lawyer has the consent of the other lawyer or is authorized to do so by law or a court order.

NORTH DAKOTA RULE OF PROFESSIONAL CONDUCT 4.3:

Dealing with Unrepresented Person

In dealing on behalf of a client with a person who is not represented by counsel, a lawyer shall not state or imply that the lawyer is disinterested. When the lawyer knows or reasonably should know that the unrepresented person misunderstands the lawyer's role in the matter, the lawyer shall make reasonable efforts to correct the misunderstanding. The lawyer shall not give legal advice to an unrepresented person, other than the advice to secure counsel, if the lawyer knows or reasonably should know that the interests of such a person are or have a reasonable possibility of being in conflict with the interests of the client.

KANSAS RULE OF PROFESSIONAL CONDUCT 4.4:

Respect for Rights of Third Persons

(a) In representing a client, a lawyer shall not use means that have no substantial purpose other than to embarrass, delay, or burden a third person, or use methods of obtaining evidence that violate the legal rights of such a person.

(b) A lawyer who receives a document relating to the representation of the lawyer's client and knows or reasonably should know that the document was inadvertently sent shall promptly notify the sender.

NEVADA RULE OF PROFESSIONAL CONDUCT 8.4:

Misconduct

It is professional misconduct for a lawyer to:

(a) Violate or attempt to violate the Rules of Professional Conduct, knowingly assist or induce another to do so, or do so through the acts of another;

(b) Commit a criminal act that reflects adversely on the lawyer's honesty, trustworthiness or fitness as a lawyer in other respects;

(c) Engage in conduct involving dishonesty, fraud, deceit or misrepresentation;

(d) Engage in conduct that is prejudicial to the administration of justice;

(e) State or imply an ability to influence improperly a government agency or official or to achieve results by means that violate the Rules of Professional Conduct or other law; or

(f) Knowingly assist a judge or judicial officer in conduct that is a violation of applicable rules of judicial conduct or other law.

APPENDIX 4:
WHERE TO FIND STATE LAWYER RULES
OF PROFESSIONAL CONDUCT

STATE	WEBSITE
Alabama	http://www.alabar.org/public/ropc.cfm
Alaska	http://www.state.ak.us/courts/prof.htm
Arizona	http://www.myazbar.org/Ethics/rules.cfm
Arkansas	http://courts.state.ar.us/rules/index2.html#Conduct
California	http://www.calbar.ca.gov/state/calbar/calbar_generic.jsp?cid=10158&id=3422
Colorado	http://www.cobar.org/Docs/New%20Colo%20RPC%20eff%201-1-08.pdf
Connecticut	http://www.jud.ct.gov/Publications/PracticeBook/pb1.pdf#page=9
Delaware	http://courts.delaware.gov/Rules/?FinalDLRPCclean.pdf
District of Columbia	http://www.dcbar.org/new_rules/index.cfm
Florida	http://www.floridabar.org/divexe/rrtfb.nsf/WContents?OpenView&Start=1&Count=30&Expand=4
Georgia	http://www.gabar.org/handbook/part_iv_after_january_1_2001_-_georgia_rules_of_professional_conduct/
Hawaii	http://www.state.hi.us/jud/ctrules/hrpcond.htm
Idaho	http://www.isc.idaho.gov/irpc0304_cov.htm
Illinois	http://www.state.il.us/court/SupremeCourt/Rules/Art_VIII/

STATE	WEBSITE
Indiana	http://www.state.in.us/judiciary/rules/prof_conduct/index.html
Iowa	http://www.judicial.state.ia.us/Professional_Regulation/Rules_of_Professional_Conduct/
Kansas	http://www.kscourts.org/ctruls/Rule226_new070107.pdf
Kentucky	http://www.kybar.org/Default.aspx?tabid=237
Louisiana	http://www.ladb.org/Publications/ropc2006-04-01.pdf
Maine	http://www.mebaroverseers.org/Home/Code%20of%20Professional%20Responsibility.html
Maryland	http://www.courts.state.md.us/rules/rodocs/153ro.pdf
Massachusetts	http://www.mass.gov/obcbbo/rpcnet.htm
Michigan	http://www.michbar.org/generalinfo/pdfs/mrpc.pdf
Minnesota	http://www.courts.state.mn.us/lprb/rules.html
Mississippi	http://www.mssc.state.ms.us/rules/RuleContents.asp?IDNum=7
Missouri	http://www.courts.mo.gov/page.asp?id=707
Montana	http://www.montanabar.org/attyrulesandregs/pdfs/rpc.pdf
Nebraska	http://www.supremecourt.ne.gov/rules/pdf/rulesprofconduct-34.pdf
Nevada	http://www.leg.state.nv.us/CourtRules/RPC.html
New Hampshire	http://www.courts.state.nh.us/rules/pcon/index.htm
New Jersey	http://www.judiciary.state.nj.us/rules/apprpc.htm
New Mexico	http://www.conwaygreene.com/nmsu/lpext.dll?f=templates&fn=main-hit-h.htm&2.0 [New Mexico Statutes and Court Rules → Contents of Judicial Volumes → Rules of Professional Conduct]
New York	http://www.nysba.org/Content/NavigationMenu/Attorney_Resources/Lawyers_Code_of_Professional_Responsibility/Lawyers.Code.pdf
North Carolina	http://www.ncbar.com/rules/rpcsearch.asp
North Dakota	http://www.court.state.nd.us/rules/conduct/contents.htm
Ohio	http://www.sconet.state.oh.us/Atty-Svcs/ProfConduct/default.asp
Oklahoma	http://www.oscn.net/applications/oscn/index.asp?ftdb=STOKRUPR&level=1

STATE	WEBSITE
Oregon	http://www.osbar.org/_docs/rulesregs/orpc.pdf
Pennsylvania	http://www.pacode.com/secure/data/204/chapter81/s81.4.html
Rhode Island	http://www.courts.state.ri.us/supreme/disciplinary/rulesof-professionalconduct.htm
South Carolina	http://www.judicial.state.sc.us/courtReg/newrules/NewRules.cfm
South Dakota	http://www.sdbar.org/Rules/Rules/PC_Rules.htm
Tennessee	http://www.tba.org/ethics/index.html
Texas	http://www.txethics.org/reference_rules.asp?view=conduct
Utah	http://www.utcourts.gov/resources/rules/ucja/index.htm#Chapter%2013
Vermont	http://www.vermontjudiciary.org/PRB1.htm
Virginia	http://www.vsb.org/docs/rules-pc_2006-07pg.pdf
Washington	http://www.courts.wa.gov/court_rules/?fa=court_rules.list&group=ga&set=RPC
West Virginia	http://www.wvbar.org/BARINFO/rulesprofconduct/index.htm
Wisconsin	http://www.legis.state.wi.us/rsb/scr/5200.pdf
Wyoming	http://courts.state.wy.us/CourtRules_Entities.aspx?RulesPage =AttorneysConduct.xml

APPENDIX 5:
TABLE OF STATE DISCIPLINARY AGENCIES

Note: If you have questions or concerns about your lawyer, you can learn more by contacting the disciplinary agency listed for your state below.

STATE	DISCIPLINARY AGENCY	MAILING ADDRESS	PHONE & FAX NUMBERS	WEBSITE
Alabama	Alabama State Bar Office of the General Counsel	P.O. Box 671 Montgomery, AL 36104	Phone: 334.269.1515 Fax: 334.261.6311	http://www.alabar.org/ogc/
Alaska	Alaska Bar Association	P.O. Box 100279 Anchorage, AK 99510-0279	Phone: 907.272.7469 Fax: 907.272.2932	http://www.alaskabar.org/index.cfm?id=4852

STATE	DISCIPLINARY AGENCY	MAILING ADDRESS	PHONE & FAX NUMBERS	WEBSITE
Arizona	Lawyer Regulation Department of the State Bar of Arizona	4201 North 24th Street Suite 200 Phoenix, AZ 85016	Phone: 602.340.7280 Fax: 602.271.4930	http://www.azbar.org/WorkingWithLawyers/menu.cfm
Arkansas	Office of the Arkansas Supreme Ct. Committee on Professional Conduct	625 Marshall Stree t110 Justice Building Little Rock, AK 72201	Phone: 501.376.0313 800.506.6631 Fax: 501.376.3438	http://courts.state.ar.us/courts/cpc.html
California	Attorney Discipline System of the State Bar of California	1149 South Hill Street Los Angeles, CA 90015	Phone: 213.765.1468 Fax: 213.765.1029	http://www.calbar.ca.gov/state/calbar/calbar_generic.jsp?cid=10179&id=1139
Colorado	Colorado Supreme Ct. - Attorney Regulation Counsel	1560 BroadwaySuite 1800Denver, CO 80202	Phone: 303.866.6400 877.888.1370	http://www.coloradosupremecourt.com/Regulation/Regulation.asp
Connecticut	Statewide Grievance Committee	287 Main StreetSecond FloorSuite Two East Hartford, CT 06118-1885	Phone: 860.568.5157 Fax: 860.568.4953	http://www.jud.ct.gov/SGC/

STATE	DISCIPLINARY AGENCY	MAILING ADDRESS	PHONE & FAX NUMBERS	WEBSITE
Delaware	Office of Disciplinary Counsel of the Supreme Court of Delaware	Caravel State Office Building 820 North French Street, 11th Floor Wilmington, DE 19801-3545	Phone: 302.577.7042 Fax: 302.577.7048	http://courts.delaware.gov/odc/
District of Columbia	District of Columbia Office of Bar Counsel	515 Fifth Street NW Building A, Suite 117 Washington, DC 20001	Phone: 202.638.1501 Fax: 202.638.0862	http://www.dcbar.org/for_the_public/working_with_lawyers/when_problems_arise/index.cfm
Florida	The Florida Bar - Department of Lawyer Regulation	651 E. Jefferson Street Tallahassee, FL 32399-2300	Phone: 850.561.5845	http://www.floridabar.org/tfb/TFBLawReg.nsf/E0F40AF2C23904C785256709006A3713/12E6C80E88BA08FD85256B2F006C9D15?Open Document
Georgia	State Bar of Georgia's Office of the General Counsel	104 Marietta Street Suite 100 Atlanta, GA 30303	Phone: 404.527.8720 800.334.6865 ext. 720 Fax: 404.527.8717	www.gabar.org
Hawaii	Office of Disciplinary Counsel	1132 Bishop Street Suite 300 Honolulu, HI 96813	Phone: 808.521.4591	http://www.courts.state.hi.us/page_server/Attorneys/79097C96709FE211F8EBCC4C9D.html

STATE	DISCIPLINARY AGENCY	MAILING ADDRESS	PHONE & FAX NUMBERS	WEBSITE
Idaho	Idaho State Bar Office of Bar Counsel	P.O. Box 895 Boise, ID 83701	Phone: 208.334.4500 Fax: 208.334.2764	www.idaho.gov/isb
Illinois	Attorney Registration & Disciplinary Commission of the Supreme Ct. of Illinois	One Prudential Plaza 130 East Randolph Drive Suite 1500 Chicago, IL 60601-6219	Phone: 312.565.2600 Fax: 312.565.2320	http://www.iardc.org/
Indiana	Indiana Supreme Ct. Disciplinary Commission	115 West Washington Street Suite 1165 Indianapolis, IN 46204	Phone: 317.232.1807 Fax: 317.233.0261	http://www.in.gov/judiciary/discipline/
Iowa	Attorney Discipline Board of the Iowa Supreme Ct.	Judicial Branch Building 1111 East Court Avenue Des Moines, IA 50319	Phone: 515.725.8017	http://www.judicial.state.ia.us/Professional_Regulation/Attorney_Discipline/
Kansas	Office of Kansas Disciplinary Administrator	701 Southwest Jackson Topeka, KS 66603	Phone: 785.296.2486 Fax: 785.296.6049	http://www.kscourts.org/attydisc/

STATE	DISCIPLINARY AGENCY	MAILING ADDRESS	PHONE & FAX NUMBERS	WEBSITE
Kentucky	Kentucky State Bar Office of Bar Counsel	514 West Main Street Frankfort, KY 40601-1883	Phone: 502.564.3795 Fax: 502.564.4038	http://www.kybar.org
Louisiana	The Louisiana Attorney Disciplinary Board	2800 Veterans Memorial Boulevard Suite 310 Metairie, LA 70002	Phone: 504.834.1488 800.489.8411 Fax: 504.834.1449	http://www.ladb.org
Maine	Maine Board of Overseers of the Bar	97 Winthrop Street P.O. Box 527 Augusta, ME 04332-0527	Phone: 207.623.1121 Fax: 207.623.4175	http://www.mebaroverseers.org/
Maryland	Attorney Grievance Commission of Maryland	100 Community Place Suite 3301 Crownsville, MD 21032-2027	Phone: 410.514.7051 800.492.1660 Fax: 410.987.4690	http://www.courts.state.md.us/attygrievance/
Massachusetts	Office of the Bar Counsel	99 High Street Boston, MA 02110	Phone: 617.728.8750 Fax: 617.482.2992	http://www.mass.gov/obcbbo/
Michigan	The Attorney Grievance Commission	Marquette Building 243 West Congress Suite 256 Detroit, MI 48226	Phone: 313.961.6585 Fax: 313.961.5819	http://www.agcmi.com/

STATE	DISCIPLINARY AGENCY	MAILING ADDRESS	PHONE & FAX NUMBERS	WEBSITE
Minnesota	Minnesota Office of Lawyers Professional Responsibility Board	1500 Landmark Towers 345 St. Peter Street St. Paul, MN 55102-1218	Phone: 651.296.3952 800.657.3601 Fax: 651.297.5801	http://www.mncourts.gov/lprb
Mississippi	The Mississippi State Bar	P.O. Box 2168 Jackson, MS 39225-2168	Phone: 601.948.4471 Fax: 601.355.8635	http://www.msbar.org
Missouri	Office of the Chief Disciplinary Counsel	3335 American Avenue Jefferson City, MO 65109-1079	Phone: 573.635.7400 Fax: 573.635.2240	http://www.mochiefcounsel.org/
Montana	Office of Disciplinary Counsel for the State of Montana	P.O. Box 1099 Helena, MT 59624-1099	Phone: 406.442.1648 877.442.1648 Fax: 406.442.2685	http://www.montanaodc.org/
Nebraska	Nebraska Supreme Court Counsel for Discipline	3808 Normal Boulevard Lincoln, NE 68506	Phone: 402.471.1040 Fax: 402.471.1014	http://www.nebar.com
Nevada	Discipline Department of the State Bar of Nevada	600 Charleston Boulevard Las Vegas, NV 89104	Phone: 702.382.2200 Fax: 702.385.2878	http://www.nvbar.org/ethics/ethics_overview. htm

STATE	DISCIPLINARY AGENCY	MAILING ADDRESS	PHONE & FAX NUMBERS	WEBSITE
New Hampshire	The New Hampshire Supreme Ct. Attorney Discipline Office	4 Chennell Drive Suite 102 Concord, NH 03301	Phone: 603.224.5828 Fax: 603.228.9511	http://www.courts.state.nh.us/committees/attydiscip/index.htm
New Jersey	Supreme Ct of New Jersey Office of Attorney Ethics	P.O. Box 963 Trenton, NJ 08625	Phone: 609.530.4008 Fax: 609.530.5238	http://www.judiciary.state.nj.us/oae/index.htm
New Mexico	The Disciplinary Board of the Supreme Ct. of New Mexico	P.O. Box 1809 Albuquerque, NM 87103-1809	Phone: 505.842.5781 Fax: 505.766.6833	http://www.nmdisboard.org/
New York – First Judicial Department: For Manhattan & Bronx	Departmental Disciplinary Committee	61 Broadway 2nd Floor New York, NY 10006	Phone: 212.401.0800 Fax: 212.401.0810	http://www.nycourts.gov/courts/ad1/attorney_discipline.shtml
New York – Second Judicial Department: For Brooklyn, Queens & Staten Island	Grievance Committee, 2nd & 11th Districts	Renaissance Plaza 335 Adams Street Suite 2400 Brooklyn, NY 11201	Phone: 718.923.6300 Fax: 718.624.2978	http://www.courts.state.ny.us/courts/ad2/attorneymatters_ComplaintAboutaLawyer.shtml

STATE	DISCIPLINARY AGENCY	MAILING ADDRESS	PHONE & FAX NUMBERS	WEBSITE
New York – Second Judicial Department: For Nassau & Suffolk Counties	Grievance Committee, 10th District	150 Motor Parkway Suite 102 Hauppauge, NY 11788	Phone: 631.231.3773 Fax: 516.364.7355	http://www.courts.state.ny.us/courts/ad2/ attorneymatters_ComplaintAboutaLawyer. shtml
New York – Second Judicial Department: For Westchester, Rockland, Orange, Putnam & Duchess Counties	Grievance Committee, 9th District	399 Knollwood Road Suite 200 White Plains, NY 10603	Phone: 914.949.4540 Fax: 914.949.0997	http://www.courts.state.ny.us/courts/ad2/ attorneymatters_ComplaintAboutaLawyer. shtml
New York – Third Judicial Department	Committee on Professional Standards	40 Steuben Street #502 Albany, NY 12207	Phone: 518.285.8350 Fax: 518.474.0389	http://www.nycourts.gov/ad3/cops/index.html
New York – Fourth Judicial Department: 5th District	Attorney Grievance Committee, 5th District	Syracuse Square 224 Harrison Street Suite 408 Syracuse, NY 13202-3066	Phone: 315.471.1835 Fax: 315.471.0123	http://nycourts.gov/ad4/AG/AGDefault.htm
New York – Fourth Judicial Department: 7th District	Attorney Grievance Committee, 7th District	50 East Avenue Suite 404 Rochester, NY 14604-2206	Phone: 585.546.8340 Fax: 585.530.3191	http://nycourts.gov/ad4/AG/AGDefault.htm

STATE	DISCIPLINARY AGENCY	MAILING ADDRESS	PHONE & FAX NUMBERS	WEBSITE
New York – Fourth Judicial Department: 8th District	Attorney Grievance Committee, 8th District	438 Main Street Room 800 Buffalo, NY 14202-3212	Phone: 716.858.1190 Fax: 716.856.2701	http://nycourts.gov/ad4/AG/AGDefault.htm
North Carolina	North Carolina State Bar	P.O. Box 25908 Raleigh, NC 27611-5908	Phone: 919.828.4620 Fax: 919.834.8156	http://www.ncbar.gov/public/
North Dakota	Disciplinary Board of the Supreme Court of North Dakota	600 East Boulevard Avenue Dept. 180 Bismarck, ND 58505-0530	Phone: 701.328.2221	http://www.ndcourts.gov/court/committees/disc_brd/information.htm
Ohio	Office of Disciplinary Counsel	250 Civic Center Drive Suite 325 Columbus, OH 43215-7411	Phone: 614.461.0256 800.589.5256 Fax: 614.461.7205	http://www.sconet.state.oh.us/odc/
Oklahoma	The Oklahoma Bar Association Office of the General Counsel	P.O. Box 53036 Oklahoma City, OK 73152	Phone: 405.416.7007 Fax: 405.416.7003	http://www.okbar.org/members/gencounsel/default.htm
Oregon	Oregon State Bar Disciplinary Counsel	P.O. Box 1689 Lake Oswego, OR 97035-0889	Phone: 503.620.0222 ext. 334 Fax: 503.968.4457	http://www.osbar.org/discipline/discipline.html

STATE	DISCIPLINARY AGENCY	MAILING ADDRESS	PHONE & FAX NUMBERS	WEBSITE
Pennsylvania	Disciplinary Board of the Supreme Ct. of Pennsylvania	200 North Third Street Suite 1400 Harrisburg, PA 17101	Phone: 717.783.0990 Fax: 717.783.4963	http://www.padb.us
Rhode Island	Disciplinary Board of the Supreme Ct. of Rhode Island	Fogarty Judicial Annex 24 Weybosset Street Providence, RI 02903	Phone: 401.222.3270 Fax: 401.222.1191	http://www.courts.state.ri.us/supreme/disciplinary/defaultdisciplinary.htm
South Carolina	Supreme Ct. of South Carolina Office of Disciplinary Counsel	P.O. Box 12159 Columbia, SC 29211	Phone: 803.734.2038 Fax: 803.734.1964	http://www.judicial.state.sc.us/discCounsel/index.cfm
South Dakota	Disciplinary Board of the State Bar of South Dakota	222 East Capitol Pierre, SD 57501	Phone: 605.763.2107 Fax: 605.763.2106	http://www.sdbar.org/Ethics/discipline_inc.HTM
Tennessee	Board of Professional Responsibility of the Supreme Ct. of Tennessee	1101 Kermit Drive Suite 730 Nashville, TN 37217	Phone: 615.361.7500 800.486.5714 Fax: 615.367.2480	http://www.tbpr.org

STATE	DISCIPLINARY AGENCY	MAILING ADDRESS	PHONE & FAX NUMBERS	WEBSITE
Texas	The Chief Disciplinary Counsel for the State Bar of Texas	P.O. Box 12487 Austin, TX 787111	Phone: 512.453.5535 800.204.222 Fax: 512.453.6667	http://www.texasbar.com/Template.cfm?Section=Client_Assistance_and_Grievance&Template=/TaggedPage/TaggedPageDisplay.cfm&TPLID=51&ContentID=7034
Utah	Office of Professional Conduct	645 South 200 East Suite 205 Salt Lake City, UT 84111-3834	Phone: 801.531.9110 Fax: 801.531.9912	http://www.utahbar.org/opc/Welcome.html
Vermont	Professional Responsibility Board of the Supreme Ct. of Vermont	32 Cherry Street Suite 213 Burlington, VT 05401	Phone: 802.359.3000 Fax: 802.359.3003	http://www.vermontjudiciary.org/Committes/boards/prb.htm
Virginia	Professional Regulation Dept. of the Virginia State Bar	707 E. Main St., Suite 1500 Richmond, VA 23219-2800	Phone: 804.775.0555 Fax: 804.775.0597	http://www.vsb.org/site/regulation/
Washington	Washington State Bar Association Disciplinary Board	1325 Fourth Avenue Suite 600 Seattle, WA 98101-2539	Phone: 206.727.8207 800.345.9722 Fax: 206.727.8325	http://www.wsba.org/public/complaints/default1.htm
West Virginia	Office of Disciplinary Counsel	2008 Kanawha Blvd., East Charleston, WV 25311	Phone: 304.558.7999 Fax: 304.558.4015	http://www.wvbar.org/BARINFO/ODC/main.htm

STATE	DISCIPLINARY AGENCY	MAILING ADDRESS	PHONE & FAX NUMBERS	WEBSITE
Wisconsin	Wisconsin Office of Lawyer Regulation	110 E. Main St. Suite 315 Madison, WI 53703-3383	Phone: 608.267.7274 Fax: 608.267.1959	http://www.wicourts.gov/olr
Wyoming	Bar Counsel of the Wyoming State Bar	P.O. Box 109 Cheyenne, WY 82003	Phone: 307.632.9061 Fax: 307.632.3737	http://www.wyomingbar.org

GLOSSARY:
YOUR GUIDE TO LEGAL DEFINITIONS
IN THIS BOOK

Advertising—Any **communication** you receive from a lawyer—a letter, a flyer, a website, a radio or television ad—with whom you have no prior or present relationship. Though by looking at lawyers' ads, particularly those on late night television, you might not recognize it, lawyer advertisements are highly regulated to protect you from misleading or over-exuberant self-promotion.

Alternative Dispute Resolution ("ADR")—A generic term that refers to out-of-court methods for resolving disputes. **Arbitration** and **mediation** are the most popular forms of **ADR**. These devices sometimes offer the parties greater satisfaction but they also may be just expensive way stations on the road to **litigation**, and for some clients, nothing short of a full-bore trial will provide them with complete satisfaction.

Arbitration—A less formal process for adjudicating a disputed matter generally entered into by agreement and typically presided over by one or three individuals who are often selected by the parties to the matter. **Arbitration** decisions are binding and appealable only on the most limited grounds. **Arbitration** is a favorite of parties who don't trust juries. It is also conventional wisdom that **arbitration** is less expensive than full bore **litigation**; actual experience often proves otherwise.

Billable Hour—The most common way lawyers charge for their services. Typically lawyers keep track of their time in quarters or tenths of an hour. While the **billable hour** offers a certain level of precision to the lawyer's **fee,** it also provides incentives for lawyers to dedicate lots of time to a matter. Lawyers regularly brag about how many **billable hours** they rack up; they also complain about how many **billable hours** they feel they must accumulate.

Breach of Fiduciary Duty—A violation by a lawyer of a basic **fiduciary duty**, such as **communication**, **confidentiality** or **loyalty** owed to a client that may give rise to a claim by the client against the lawyer.

Client Trust Account—The bank account maintained by your lawyer in which the lawyer maintains the safekeeping of client's property. (See also **IOLTA**.)

Communicate, Communication—A lawyer's obligation to keep you informed, so that you can define your best interests and instruct your lawyer about your objectives in the legal matter.

Competent, Competence—A lawyer's obligation to *investigate* relevant facts, *understand* relevant law, *formulate* a legal strategy that furthers your goals, and *draft* documents to implement them.

Confidentiality, Confidential Information—A lawyer's obligation to blanket everything learned in the course of a representation with complete secrecy. Your lawyer is not permitted to disclose your **confidential information** without your permission. If it hasn't been disclosed on Action News, then your lawyer should treat your information as a secret.

Conflict of Interest—A lawyer's dedication to another client, to a third person or to the lawyer's own self-interest that has the potential to compromise your lawyer's dedication to your matter. Lawyers are not permitted to proceed with a matter until they have identified and resolved **conflicts of interest** by disclosing them to clients and obtaining a client's **informed consent**, or permission to proceed. (See also **Informed Consent**.)

Conflicts Check—The inquiry a lawyer makes among his colleagues, in his files and in his own heart to determine whether there is any reason he cannot take on a particular matter because of other representations, duties to other people or entities, or any personal commitment that might interfere with his total **loyalty** to you and your matter.

Contempt—A finding by a judge that a person or organization, appearing before the court, has failed to obey an order of the court. Sometimes lawyers will risk being found in **contempt** in order to get an appellate court to review what the lawyer believes is an erroneous ruling by a court that the lawyer must reveal your privileged information.

Court Rules and Procedures—The courts issue rules and procedures that govern how matters before them should proceed. Because these rules and procedures govern the conduct of lawyers, there are constant disputes over what the rules mean and how they should be applied. Your lawyer is required to follow these rules and procedures.

Disbursements—The payments lawyers make to others (FedEx, expert witnesses, court reporters) on your behalf.

Disqualification—A sanction sometimes imposed by a court when the court determines that a lawyer is laboring under a **conflict of interest** that results in the lawyer being prohibited from continuing one or more representations. Lawyers hate to be disqualified.

Expenses—The cost of non-legal services (photocopying, electronic research) the lawyer incurs on your behalf for which she likely will seek reimbursement.

Fee, Fee Arrangement—The amount of compensation agreed upon by client and lawyer to complete a legal matter. (See also **Retainer Letter**.)

> **Blended Fee**—An agreement by lawyer and client that the lawyer will be compensated in part by an hourly or **fixed fee** and in part on a **contingent fee**.
>
> **Contingent Fee**—A fee arrangement in which a client owes no fee until she collects money. Lawyers typically charge one-quarter to 40% of a client's recovery.
>
> **Fixed Fee**—An agreement by lawyer and client that the lawyer will perform a specified scope of services for a predetermined professional fee regardless of how much time will be required to complete the task. A **fixed fee** is said to be a great incentive for a lawyer to work very fast.
>
> **Hourly Fee**—An agreement by lawyer and client that the lawyer will be compensated for whatever services the client requests based on the number of hours dedicated to the matter times the hourly rate of each lawyer and **paralegal** who worked on the matter. An **hourly fee** is said to be a great incentive for a lawyer to work very slowly.

Fee Forfeiture—A sanction that can be imposed on a lawyer in a case in which it is determined that the lawyer did not earn some or all of the **fee** received or is otherwise not entitled to retain the **fee** because of a **breach of fiduciary duty** such as failing to disclose to the client the lawyer's **conflict of interest**.

Fiduciary Duty—Your lawyer is a fiduciary, which means that she is required to put your interest ahead of hers. She owes you fiduciary duties of **competence, communication, confidentiality** and **loyalty**.

The 4 Cs—Fox and Martyn's shorthand for the four principal fiduciary duties lawyers owe their clients: **communication, competence, confidentiality** and **conflict of interest** resolution (or **loyalty**). (See also **Loyalty**.)

Fraud—Conduct that by commission or omission misleads people into believing that "X" is the truth, when in fact it is "Y." Depending on the context and the relationship of the actors, it can give rise to criminal or civil liability by the person who engaged in the misleading or untruthful conduct. Enron, Adelphia, Tyco and WorldCom are examples of serious consequences for massive **frauds**.

Informed Consent—Client consent to a course of conduct after learning from a lawyer the available options and the advantages and disadvantages of each. (See also **Conflict of Interest** and **Waiver of Conflict of Interest**.)

IOLTA—An acronym for a lawyer's trust account that means "Interest on Lawyer's Trust Accounts." Lawyers are required to keep some client funds in **IOLTA** accounts, and state law requires banks to forward the interest on the account to a statewide fund that pays for legal services to the poor. (See also **Client Trust Account**.)

Joint Clients—The representation by a lawyer of more than one client in the same matter, a situation fraught with ethical implications for the lawyer. (See also **Conflict of Interest**.)

Law Firm—A group of lawyers organized to practice law together as a partnership, limited liability company, agency or governmental office. Clients are entitled to special protections from all lawyers in a **law firm**.

Litigation—The generic name for the process of deciding civil disputes in the courts, from the filing of a complaint to the decision in the final appeal. Because most **litigation** results in settlements, we refer to the lawyers who engage in the process as litigators; trial lawyers are those few lawyers who actually get to take a matter to trial before judge or jury.

Loyalty—A lawyer's fiduciary obligation to place each client's interests above those of the lawyer or other third persons. Lawyers remain loyal by resolving **conflicts of interest**.

Malpractice—What occurs when a client is injured by conduct of the lawyer that fails to meet the standard of care the lawyer owed the client. Usually, clients need the expert testimony of another lawyer to prove the applicable standard of care, but courts often find that really obvious mistakes, like missing a filing deadline or failing to follow a client's lawful instructions, speak for themselves.

Mediation—A process presided over by a professional neutral in which the parties attempt to settle a dispute.

Paralegal—Lawyer assistants, often specially trained, who assist lawyers in the delivering of legal services by conducting factual research, organizing and reviewing documents, interviewing witnesses, and similar tasks under the control and supervision of lawyers.

Professional Discipline—The process by which it is determined whether a lawyer's conduct violates the applicable **rules of professional conduct** and, if so, what the appropriate sanction (reprimand, suspension, disbarment) might be for the violation. The public sometimes views the disciplinary process with some skepticism because the process is by and large controlled by lawyers judging other lawyers, although most states include non-lawyers on hearing panels.

Prosecutor—The lawyer who in the name of the state or federal government asserts criminal charges against individuals and organizations, and then either accepts a plea bargain or tries the case against the accused. It is said that a **prosecutor** is not interested in convictions but rather that justice is done; it is said as a result that **prosecutors** have special duties to the truth-finding process; many defense lawyers think that duty is honored in its breach.

Quantum Meruit—A method of determining the value to the client of the services provided by a lawyer who has either withdrawn or been dismissed from a representation. (See also **Withdrawal.**)

Reasonable—A fuzzy word that permits lawyers to argue on both sides of a question.

Retainer Letter—The document the lawyer should send you to describe the services the lawyer expects to provide, the basis on which the **fee** will be computed, and the terms on which you will be charged for **disbursements** and **expenses**. (See also **Fees.**)

Rules of Professional Conduct—The code adopted by each state, generally by the state supreme court, to govern the conduct of lawyers in their dealings with clients, the courts and the public.

Solicitation—The process by which a lawyer affirmatively seeks new clients and additional work from existing clients. Some forms of **solicitation** are permissible; others are not.

Specialization—Many lawyers specialize in certain matters. Lawyers, however, are not permitted to hold themselves out as specialists unless they have been certified as specialists by an approved organization with established criteria and a formal certification process.

Unrepresented Person—An individual involved in a matter as a party, witness or participant who has no lawyer. **Unrepresented persons** are entitled to special protections.

Waiver of Conflict of Interest—Your agreeing, after being fully informed of the consequences, to give up your right to object to your lawyer's **conflict of interest**. (See also **Informed Consent**.)

Withdraw or Withdrawal—The process by which a lawyer removes herself from a representation over the client's objection. There are certain situations where **withdrawal** is required, others where it is permitted, and still others where it is impermissible. Sometimes in order to **withdraw** a lawyer must seek court permission.

INDEX

A

advertising, by lawyer, 9–10, 119

advisor, lawyer as, representative state rule on, 99

aiding and abetting, 60, 62, 64

alternative dispute resolution (ADR), 3, 78, 119

ambulance chasing, 11

American Bar Association (ABA), 79

American Lawyer Referral, 80

arbitration, 3, 119

attorney-client privilege, 35–36

attorney referral services, 10–11, 79–82

authority
- allocating between client/lawyer, 85
- reserved to client, 85–86
- reserved to lawyer, 86

B

bar, admission to, 3, 4

Best Lawyers, 80

billable hour, 15, 119

buying client claims, 44

C

client trust account, 20, 120

communication with client, 25–28
- business advice, 28
- consultation, 26
- definition of communication, 120
- fiduciary duty, 5, 6
- insurance company defending case, 27–28
- lawyer errors, 28
- major strategic decisions, 27–28
- mistakes by lawyer, 28
- as one of 4 C's, 3, 5, 121
- periodic reports, 25
- questions to ask lawyer, 27

How to Deal With Your Lawyer